1982

NEW DIRECTIONS
FOR CONTINUING
EDUCATION

Number 8 • 1980

NEW DIRECTIONS FOR CONTINUING EDUCATION

A Quarterly Sourcebook
Alan B. Knox, Editor-in-Chief

Number 8, 1980

Reaching Hard-to-Reach Adults

Gordon G. Darkenwald
Gordon A. Larson
Guest Editors

Jossey-Bass Inc., Publishers
San Francisco • Washington • London

REACHING HARD-TO-REACH ADULTS
New Directions for Continuing Education
Number 8, 1980
      Gordon G. Darkenwald, Gordon A. Larson, Guest Editors

New Directions for Continuing Education (publication number
0195-2242) quarterly by Jossey-Bass Inc., Publishers.
Subscriptions are available at the regular rate for institutions,
libraries, and agencies of $30 for one year. Individuals may
subscribe at the special professional rate of $18 for one year.

Correspondence:
Subscriptions, single-issue orders, change of address notices,
undelivered copies, and other correspondence should be sent to
New Directions Subscriptions, Jossey-Bass Inc., Publishers,
433 California Street, San Francisco, California 94104.

Editorial correspondence should be sent to the Editor-in-Chief,
Alan B. Knox, Office for the Study of Continuing Professional
Education, University of Illinois at Urbana–Champaign,
Urbana, Illinois 61801.

Library of Congress Catalogue Card Number LC 79-89390

International Standard Serial Number ISSN 0195-2242

International Standard Book Number ISBN 87589-815-7

Cover design by Willi Baum

Manufactured in the United States of America

Contents

Editors' Notes

Continuing educators seldom have a guaranteed clientele. For the most part, we must persuade adults to participate in our programs and adapt the delivery of education to their needs and circumstances. We must *reach* adults through appropriate marketing and recruitment strategies, programming methods, and delivery systems.

As every continuing educator knows, however, certain segments of the adult population are difficult to reach. Why this is so and what can be done about it are crucial questions for most of us in the field. Consequently, the purpose of this volume is to define and describe hard-to-reach adult populations, to identify the major obstacles to their participation in continuing education, to review and interpret the relevant research and theory, and to illustrate approaches to reaching the hard-to-reach that have been used successfully by different agencies for a variety of target groups and purposes.

While all the chapters discuss both research and practical applications, the first three emphasize basic conceptualizations and research findings, and the next three stress concrete strategies for reaching specific hard-to-reach groups. In the first chapter, which serves as a general introduction, Darkenwald reviews theory and research on participation in continuing education and highlights concepts and findings relevant to the hard-to-reach learner. In the second chapter, Beder shows the utility of marketing concepts and techniques to the continuing education administrator concerned with overcoming resistance to participation. In the third chapter, Larson emphasizes how an understanding of communication processes can help continuing educators stimulate awareness and interest among potential participants. He also discusses communications technology, particularly in reference to innovative delivery systems. The next three chapters focus on hard-to-reach populations of concern to continuing educators in many types of agencies and settings. In discussing the disadvantaged adult, Irish considers lessons learned through large-scale demonstration projects that employed innovative recruitment and programming techniques. A very different target population is addressed in the following chapter. The hard-to-reach professional poses special challenges, which—as Scanlan, using the health professions as a model, shows—have often been met in highly creative ways. Reaching older adults is the topic of the sixth chapter. Spencer places particular emphasis on the need for multifaceted approaches to overcoming the barriers that discourage participation by this group. In the final chapter, the editors summarize and synthesize the differing perspectives and action recommendations presented in the previous chapters.

Gordon G. Darkenwald
Gordon A. Larson
Guest Editors

*Gordon G. Darkenwald is associate professor of adult education
and continuing education and codirector, Center for Adult
Development, Graduate School of Education, Rutgers University.
He is coauthor of* Last Gamble on Education *and other
studies related to participation in continuing education
and is a former editor of the journal* Adult Education.

*Gordon A. Larson is assistant professor of adult education and
reading and codirector, Center for Adult Development,
Graduate School of Education, Rutgers University. Before
coming to Rutgers, he spent fourteen years on active duty
with the U.S. Army, where he designed and implemented
an occupational literacy program that has been adopted
as the model for army basic skills education.*

*To effectively serve hard-to-reach adults, we must understand
who they are, why they should be served, and what barriers
impede their participation.*

Continuing Education and
the Hard-to-Reach Adult

Gordon G. Darkenwald

Providing a general framework for the chapters that follow, this chapter begins by defining the "hard-to-reach" adult and discusses why
reaching these potential participants is important to continuing educators. Subsequent sections analyze the sociodemographic factors that
affect participation in continuing education, and consider the principal
barriers to participation in organized adult learning activities. The
chapter concludes with a brief discussion of theoretical models of participation and their implications for professionals concerned with effectively reaching the hard-to-reach.

The Hard-to-Reach

On the most general level, the hard-to-reach are those adults
who are underrepresented in continuing education. Using this statistical criterion, the hard-to-reach include the elderly, the disadvantaged,
blue-collar workers, the handicapped, the geographically isolated, and
many other identifiable groups and subgroups in the general population. The hard-to-reach are not, however, only those who are underrepresented among participants generally. Any group of adults that a
particular agency wishes to serve but is having difficulty recruiting can
be considered hard to reach. What is important is that some group of

potential participants is not engaged in educational activity to the extent deemed feasible or desirable. Usually, though not always, the hard-to-reach are a subset of a continuing education agency's clientele. For example, a continuing medical education agency may be very successful in reaching general practitioners, but may experience great difficulty in persuading medical specialists to participate in its programs. Similarly, the training department of a large corporation may have little trouble interesting middle managers in its programs, but encounter considerable resistance from top-level executives. Sometimes a continuing education agency experiences difficulty in reaching any of its clientele. Usually, such agencies have a specific mandate to serve a narrow and difficult-to-reach target population—for example, older adults, illiterates, or the structurally unemployed. In general, however, it is neither accurate nor useful to consider an agency's entire clientele to be hard to reach. Traditional approaches to promotion and publicity, when competently employed, usually suffice to reach most adult learners. It is the exceptions that concern us in this volume.

Why Reach the Hard-to-Reach?

There are at least three reasons why reaching the hard-to-reach adult is important for continuing educators. The first has to do with social justice in the context of equal educational opportunity. The principal concern, as Anderson and Darkenwald (1979a, p. 1) have noted, is to see that "all Americans, regardless of race, age, sex, and socioeconomic status, have equal access to the education and training opportunities that help to promote social mobility, economic independence, and individual and social well-being." Continuing educators, therefore, have an ethical responsibility to serve those segments of the adult population that are underrepresented in the ranks of participants. A second basic reason for attempting to serve the hard-to-reach concerns agency self-interest. What constitutes self-interest varies so greatly from one agency to another that only a few examples can be given here. Success in reaching the hard-to-reach can benefit at least some agencies in the following ways: increasing enrollments; building goodwill and wider support; more effectively or completely accomplishing agency goals; more fully utilizing resources (funds, facilities, and so on); broadening the agency's clientele base; and enhancing the agency's reputation for expertise and accomplishment. While the self-interest of most agencies is probably clear, some may be unaware of the benefits that could accrue from a concerted effort to recruit hard-to-reach adult learners. A third reason for attempting to reach the hard-to-reach has always been uppermost in the minds of dedicated continuing educators: by and large, the hard-to-reach are those most in need of continuing education.

Who Are the Hard-to-Reach?

A number of studies have compared the characteristics of adult and continuing education participants with those of nonparticipants (Anderson and Darkenwald, 1979a; Anderson and Darkenwald, 1979b; Carp, Peterson, and Roelfs, 1974; Cross, 1979; Johnstone and Rivera, 1965). Taken as a whole, the research provides a fairly complete picture of the hard-to-reach adult learner. In the description that follows, only the most important factors distinguishing participants from nonparticipants are considered. They are summarized in three categories, relating to social status, age, and geographical isolation.

Low-SES Adults. Socioeconomic status (SES) is typically assessed on the basis of three factors: educational attainment (amount of formal schooling), occupational status, and income. Most continuing educators know that low-SES adults are harder than other adults to reach—and to retain—in continuing education programs of any kind. Low SES, of course, is related to other characteristics, such as race and ethnicity. It is important, however, to distinguish between these factors and SES. The research evidence (Anderson and Darkenwald, 1979a) makes clear that race in itself does not distinguish between participants and nonparticipants in continuing education. When race is "controlled" by SES (for example, by comparing participation rates for high-SES blacks with rates for high-SES whites), there is even a slight tendency for minorities to participate more than whites. SES is the single most powerful predictor of participation in continuing education. Its effects can be viewed as operating in a uniform way, much like the mercury in a thermometer. As SES drops, degree by degree, so does the likelihood of participation in continuing education. When SES hovers near the bottom of the scale, the probability of participation is virtually nil.

While the components of SES tend to be highly interrelated (for example, people with little schooling tend to have low-status jobs and low incomes), this is not always the case, nor does it logically follow that all three components should affect participation equally. Recent statistical analyses of a national data base (Anderson and Darkenwald, 1979a) show that educational attainment has a stronger association with participation than does occupational status, and both of these factors are more potent than income in predicting participation. Thus the hardest-to-reach low-SES adults are those with the least formal schooling, not necessarily those with the lowest incomes. The importance of educational attainment is graphically underscored by comparing the national participation rate of adults with eleven years of schooling or less with the rate of participation of those with four years of college or more. In the former case, only 3.3 percent participated in 1975, compared with a participation rate of 28.3 percent for college graduates (National Center for Education Statistics, 1978).

Older Adults. Age is another factor that has a pronounced, negative association with participation in continuing education. The participation rate for young adults aged seventeen to thirty-four is nearly four times as great as the rate of participation for those fifty-five and older (National Center for Education Statistics, 1978). As with SES, a thermometer-like dynamic seems operative. With every added year the likelihood of participation by an older adult diminishes further. Participation by adults over seventy-five is virtually negligible. The low rate of participation by older people is to some extent intertwined with SES: old people, like racial and ethnic minorities, tend on the average to be poorer and less educated than the general population. Nevertheless, when SES is controlled statistically, by comparing, for example, high-SES older adults with high-SES younger adults, the participation rate for older people is still substantially lower. Of course, the hardest-to-reach old people, like the hardest to reach in any category, are those who suffer the greatest socioeconomic handicaps.

Isolated Adults. Adults who, for some reason or another, lack ready access to educational resources are less likely than the nonisolated to participate in continuing education. Isolation can result from many factors, including chronic illness or physical handicap. For adults in general, however, geographical factors play an especially prominent role in facilitating or impeding engagement in organized learning activities. As one would expect, participation rates are notably lower in small towns and rural areas than in cities and suburbs, where access is easier and educational resources more highly concentrated (Johnstone and Rivera, 1965). Regional differences also exist, with participation rates higher in the West than in other parts of the country. Anderson and Darkenwald (1979a) attribute this latter finding to the fact that West Coast states, particularly California with its 104 community colleges, provide greater access than most other states to low-cost, publicly supported continuing education.

To recapitulate, the hardest-to-reach adults, in general, are the socioeconomically disadvantaged, the elderly, and the geographically isolated. Moreover, if we examine SES closely, it is apparent that low educational attainment is a particularly significant characteristic of the hard-to-reach learner. These findings raise some difficult and important questions. It is not completely self-evident, for example, why people with little formal schooling or older people should participate less fully in further education. On the contrary, it might be reasoned that both groups are in need of continuing education and therefore should be eager to participate in educational activities. Clearly, however, there are barriers of many kinds that operate to hinder participation on the part of these and other hard-to-reach segments of the adult population. The following section discusses these barriers.

Barriers to Participation

Several national studies (Carp, Peterson, and Roelfs, 1974; Johnstone and Rivera, 1965; Mezirow, Darkenwald, and Knox, 1975) have addressed the question of what prevents so many adults from participating in organized learning activities. When asked, adults give an amazing variety of reasons for not participating in continuing education. Most, if not all, of these reasons can be classified into informational, situational, institutional, and attitudinal barriers. The first category of barrier relates to lack of information concerning educational opportunities for adults, the second to the constraints of their individual situations, the third to obstacles erected by educational institutions, and the last to social and psychological factors that inhibit participation.

Informational Barriers. A necessary condition for participation in continuing education is awareness of educational resources in the community (Darkenwald, 1980). Unfortunately, such awareness is not as widespread as might be assumed. Some years ago Johnstone and Rivera (1965) found that one-third of all adults had no knowledge whatever of educational resources for adults in their communities. More recent studies suggest that the situation has not appreciably changed. In 1979, Cross (p. 126) concluded that about one-fourth of the adult population "do not know where to go or whom to ask to get information about learning opportunities." As might be expected, levels of awareness vary greatly in relation to such factors as socioeconomic status and place of residence. Low-SES adults, and those living in rural areas, are particularly likely to be unaware of adult learning opportunities or sources of information about them.

Situational Barriers. In some respects, this is a catchall category for a wide range of barriers related to one's general life situation: income, health, family responsibilities, work obligations, place of residence, and so on. Typical situational barriers include childcare needs, shift or overtime work, lack of transportation, poor health, and lack of time or money. Clearly, many of these situational barriers are more formidable for low-SES adults, the elderly, and other hard-to-reach subgroups than for average, middle-class adults who have more resources at their disposal.

Institutional Barriers. The special needs, problems, and concerns of mature learners are sometimes ignored or at least not recognized by organizations that provide education to the adult public. This seems particularly true of traditional providers such as schools and colleges. Cross (1979) has noted that organizations often "exclude or discourage certain groups of learners because of such things as inconvenient schedules, full-time fees for part-time study, restrictive locations, and the like" (p. 106). Other organizational barriers include lack of appropriate or relevant offerings for adult learners and policies and procedures (red tape, rigid requirements, and so on) that impose inconvenience, confusion, or frustration on potential participants. On the whole, organizational barriers are probably less severe impediments to continuing education than other kinds of barriers. However, their effects are probably felt most by those adults least proficient in coping with bureaucratic organizations—the poor, the undereducated, the foreign-born, and other hard-to-reach groups.

Attitudinal Barriers. Not surprisingly, intangible barriers are for many people much more formidable than tangible ones. How individuals think about themselves, their world, and the uses of education profoundly influences their dispositions and actions regarding continuing education. Attitudinal barriers are individually and collectively held beliefs, values, attitudes, or perceptions that inhibit participation in organized learning activities. Such notions as "schools are for children," "education is impractical," "learning is dull or difficult," "the classroom is a place of failure and humiliation," and many others are firmly held by a great many adults, particularly from blue-collar or low-SES backgrounds. Attitudinal barriers tend to focus either on education as an entity "out there" or on the self as a potential participant. Thus, adults sometimes denigrate or devalue their abilities (for example, "I'm too old, too dumb, too insecure"), education itself ("it's boring, useless, for 'eggheads'"), or both. That many of these negative beliefs and perceptions are distorted or simply false does not by any means lessen their impact, particularly when they are supported by peer-group and subcultural value systems, as is often the case among low-SES and blue-collar segments of the population. Middle- and upper-SES adults are not only less likely to denigrate their own abilities or the value of continuing education but also less likely to find support in the workplace, family, or community for negative dispositions toward learning (Johnstone and Rivera, 1965).

All of the barriers discussed here are obviously more important for those groups previously characterized as especially hard to reach—the isolated, the elderly, and those at the bottom of the social-class ladder, who have little formal education, menial or no jobs, and relatively low incomes. It is important to remember, however, that low SES and other social handicaps provide only a partial explanation for why some adults are harder to reach than others. Participation behavior is complex and our understanding of it still rudimentary. What is particularly lacking in the literature are theories or models of the participation process which can give us a deeper understanding of the factors that influence participation, how they are related to one another, and how they operate to affect actual behavior. The principal efforts to date to conceptualize participation in continuing education are summarized briefly below.

Models of Participation

The models discussed share a common assumption: participation in continuing education is the result of complex interactions involving both social and psychological factors. In every case, therefore, the focus is on both individual actors and the forces in their environments that impede or facilitate participation in continuing education.

The Economic Model. Economists tend to put particular emphasis on individual rationality in making decisions. Under some circumstances, as Dhanidina and Griffith (1975) point out, economic concepts can be useful in explaining participation in education that has "human capital investment" rather than consumptive value. Investing in one's human capital involves acquiring credentials or proficiencies that can enhance one's earning power. Assuming people act rationally, they will invest in continuing education when the benefits of such an investment are perceived to be greater than the costs. Costs include not only direct outlays for tuition, books, and so on, but also the economic value of time spent on education. Time is the principal "opportunity cost" for most adults. When this opportunity cost is low (for example, during periods of high unemployment) the economic model predicts an increase in educational participation.

The Force Field Model. Miller (1967) first suggested the use of "force field analysis" as a way of predicting participation in continuing education. Put simply, participation is seen as dependent upon the relative strength of positive versus negative forces that affect individual behavior. Certain of these forces are social or environmental, while others are individual or psychological. Miller (1967, p. 21) provides an illustration by analyzing the forces affecting participation by lower-lower-class adults. He identifies four positive forces, the first of which he considers the strongest: survival needs; changing technology; safety needs of female culture; and governmental attempts to change opportunity structure. Pitted against these positive forces are five negative forces, the first two of which are deemed especially potent: action-excitement orientation of male culture; hostility to education and to middle-class object-orientation; relative absence of specific, immediate job opportunities at end of training; limited access through organizational ties; and weak family structure. Because negative forces predominate over positive ones, both in relative potency and in number, the force field analysis predicts minimal participation by lower-lower-class adults. Interventions aimed at reducing the negative forces or enhancing the positive ones could, of course, result in reversing the prediction.

The Congruence Model. Boshier (1973) has proposed a congruence model based on self theory, which stresses the interaction between internal (psychological) and external (environmental) variables. The model, as Boshier describes it, is complex. Basically, however, it "asserts that 'congruence' both within the participant and between the participant and his educational environment determines participation/nonparticipation and dropout/persistence" (p. 256). The principal conclusion from Boshier's analysis appears to be that lower-SES adults (who in general are deficiency- as opposed to growth-motivated) are especially likely to experience "intra-self incongruence, which in turn leads to self/other incongruence and dissatisfaction with the educational environment" (p. 259). In short, according to Boshier, most low-SES adults exhibit characteristics that are incompatible with formal educational environments.

The Expectancy-Valence Model. The Swedish adult education researcher Kjell Rubenson (1977) has proposed a model of participation based on expectancy-valence theory. His formulation is elaborate and therefore will be treated here only in its barest outlines. Valence denotes a positive or negative affective attitude toward the outcome of an action, such as participation, and expectancy a belief concerning the probability that an action will result in a particular outcome. Participation in continuing education is determined jointly by valence and expectancy. For example, an expectant mother is likely to value positively a course in childbirth preparation because it promises to satisfy a need she considers important. She may also believe that she is able to participate in and complete the course and thereby achieve the desired benefits. Thus, in this example, expectancy, like valence, is highly positive and the probability of participation high. However, it would be nil if the mother-to-be placed no value on the course or if she believed that for some reason she could not participate in it. Rubenson's model posits further that expectancy and valence are determined by both individual and social/environmental variables and their interactions. Low SES would tend to affect both valence and expectancy negatively. Attitudes toward continuing education are likely to be less positive among low-SES adults and tangible obstacles to participation more numerous and formidable.

Implications

The implications of the economic model for continuing educators are straightforward: if you want to maximize participation in education (of the human capital kind), reduce costs or increase the benefits to be derived from participation. In general, the most effective way to reduce costs is to reduce the amount of time the individual must invest in education or training. Alternatively, one can target recruitment efforts on those individuals, such as the unemployed or the unskilled, for whom time has minimal economic value.

The implications of the other three models are much less clear because they involve more variables that interact in complex ways. They do, nonetheless, share one common assumption: that participation is determined jointly by individual and social/environmental factors. From this perspective, the decision to engage in education is more like choosing a marriage partner than selecting a pair of socks. The analogy is not at all frivolous if we take it a little farther and consider the way continuing educators typically market their services. Are the brochures and catalogs aimed at persuading adults to enroll in a course or workshop much different from the advertising vehicles used to sell socks? That there is little difference is not necessarily an indictment of continuing education. As Miller (1967) put it: "So long as the adult educator confronts a situation in which both personal need and social force move together toward the educational satisfaction of some need, it is relatively efficient to employ a marketplace technique. . . . A strong and visible demand is met by providing an adequate supply through some impersonal marketing device such as a catalog or newspaper announcement. Those who are sensitized by need respond individually . . . and appear at the appropriate supply source" (p. 14).

If, as Miller asserts, the traditional marketing approach works well in most instances, it clearly does not work for those adults whom we have characterized as hard to reach. Continuing educators, therefore, must devise alternative strategies for reaching the hard-to-reach when conventional marketing techniques are inadequate.

The traditional approach to marketing assumes that there are no major barriers to participation, that taking a course or engaging in some other learning activity is much like purchasing a pair of socks. For the hard-to-reach, however, we must assume just the opposite, that barriers of many kinds — attitudinal, situational, informational, institutional — severely constrain participation in organized learning activities.

Many of the more tangible barriers can be and often are attacked head-on by experienced continuing educators. Childcare facilities are established, classes are offered in convenient locations in the community, transportation is provided for older people, the electronic media are used to reach the isolated, and so on. But what of the less tangible barriers, the fears, doubts, suspicions, and misconceptions about learning that prevent so many adults from continuing their education? The answers are not so easily deduced, but the research suggests that ways must be found to convey information through personal rather than impersonal means, to utilize peer, membership, and reference

10

groups to heighten rather than dampen educational aspirations, and above all to adjust programs and services to meet the real, present needs of people.

A recent report (Hunter and Harmon, 1979) suggests that reaching the very hardest to reach may ultimately require radical departures not only in recruitment strategies but in the ways continuing educators see their roles and carry out educational programs. To reach the severely disadvantaged may necessitate the abandonment of the schooling model of continuing education and its replacement by loosely structured, nonformal strategies aimed at integrating learning with the groups, activities, and concerns of everyday life in the home, community, and workplace.

References

Anderson, R. E., and Darkenwald, G. G. *Participation and Persistence in American Adult Education.* New York: The College Board, 1979a.

Anderson, R. E., and Darkenwald, G. G. "The Adult Part-Time Learner in Colleges and Universities: A Clientele Analysis." *Research in Higher Education,* 1979b, *10* (4), 357–370.

Boshier, R. W. "Educational Participation and Dropout: A Theoretical Model." *Adult Education,* 1973, *23* (4), 255–282.

Carp, A., Peterson, R., and Roelfs, P. "Adult Learning Interests and Experiences." In K. P. Cross and J. Valley and Associates (Eds.), *Planning Non-Traditional Programs: An Analysis of the Issues for Postsecondary Education.* San Francisco: Jossey-Bass, 1974.

Cross, K. P. "Adult Learners: Characteristics, Needs, and Interests." In R. E. Peterson and Associates (Eds.), *Lifelong Learning in America: An Overview of Current Practices, Available Resources, and Future Prospects.* San Francisco: Jossey-Bass, 1979.

Darkenwald, G. G. "Educational and Career Guidance for Adults: Delivery System Alternatives." *Vocational Guidance Quarterly,* 1980, *28* (3), 200–207.

Dhanidina, L., and Griffith, W. S. "Costs and Benefits of Delayed High School Completion." *Adult Education,* 1975, *25* (4), 217–230.

Hunter, C., and Harmon, D. *Adult Illiteracy in the United States.* New York: McGraw-Hill, 1979.

Johnstone, J., and Rivera, R. *Volunteers for Learning: A Study of the Educational Pursuits of American Adults.* Chicago: Aldine, 1965.

Mezirow, J., Darkenwald, G. G., and Knox, A. *Last Gamble on Education: Dynamics of Adult Basic Education.* Washington, D.C.: Adult Education Association, 1975.

Miller, H. L. *Participation of Adults in Education: A Force Field Analysis.* Boston: Center for the Study of Liberal Education for Adults, 1967.

National Center for Education Statistics. *Participation in Adult Education: Final Report, 1975.* Washington, D.C.: U.S. Government Printing Office, 1978.

Rubenson, K. *Participation in Recurrent Education.* Paris: Center for Educational Research and Innovation, Organization for Economic Cooperation and Development, 1977.

Gordon G. Darkenwald is associate professor of adult and continuing education and codirector, Center for Adult Development, Graduate School of Education, Rutgers University.

Marketing is a total strategy for program development
in which all relevant factors are carefully orchestrated
for maximum impact on hard-to-reach target groups.

Reaching the Hard-to-Reach Adult Through Effective Marketing

Harold W. Beder

The concept of "hard to reach" has two defining elements. The first is that the hard-to-reach constitute an identifiable population that the continuing education agency desires to serve. The second is that participation of the hard-to-reach is unlikely unless specific measures are undertaken to stimulate it. In regard to marketing, Kotler (1975) suggests that it is an approach to program planning and development in which all elements of the program are manipulated to inform, motivate, and meet the needs of clients or customers. Crucial elements for manipulation are price, place, promotion, and product. Central to this definition is that marketing is a total approach to program development, in which every aspect of the program is purposefully organized to create maximum client satisfaction. Marketing should not be confused with advertising, which is but one of many marketing techniques.

In marketing, the relationship between the continuing education program and the client is considered to be one of exchange, whereby the client gives something of value—time or money, for example—for something valued equally or more, such as learning. The more value the client receives in proportion to what is given up, the more likely are participation and persistence. Consequently, marketing seeks to provide the greatest value possible to the client per unit of organizational effort. If used effectively, both the program and the learner benefit. The program becomes more successful by virtue of the fact that more clients are served to their satisfaction, while clients benefit because they gain maximum value for their efforts.

To provide maximum value to clients, at least three basic conditions must be met. First, the program must address the needs of the client. Second, the clients must be informed of the program's existence. Last, the program must express its ability to meet client needs in a fashion that motivates participation.

That all elements of the program must be manipulated for client satisfaction is one way of stating that the marketing approach requires a client-centered orientation, whether the client is an individual, a group of individuals, or an organization. To price, place, promotion, and product, Lauffler (1977) adds a fifth component—partners. From a narrow perspective, price is the amount of money charged by the program for participation. Conceived more broadly, however, price consists of the total value of all things foregone by the client to participate. Place pertains to the physical setting of the education, while promotion pertains to all efforts to inform the public and motivate participation. Product relates to the nature of the education delivered. Lauffler defines partners as "the effective use of consumers and others as active partners in addressing the above-mentioned concerns [price, place, promotion, product]" (p. 151).

Marketing Analysis

Having briefly dealt with basic marketing concepts, let us focus now on their application to the problem addressed here. The first step in employing marketing as a strategy for reaching hard-to-reach adults is market analysis, a process of analyzing the continuing education market and the forces that shape it.

At the heart of market analysis is market segmentation, defined by Kotler (1975) as "dividing the market into fairly homogeneous parts where any part may conceivably be selected as a market target to be reached with a distinct marketing mix" (p. 99). Market segmentation is fundamental to marketing practice because it recognizes that different groupings of clients are likely to respond to the program's efforts in different ways. By segmenting or grouping potential participants into categories based on how we expect them to respond to the program, the program can be adjusted in a manner appropriate to each category.

For the purpose of this discussion, let us assume that the hardest-to-reach represent a distinct market segment we wish to address—for whatever reason. To gain an understanding of how a continuing education program might optimally manipulate price, promotion, place, product, and partners to serve the hardest-to-reach, it is first necessary to determine what characteristics they share and on what dimensions various subgroupings differ. A reluctance or inability to participate is by definition a characteristic the hardest-to-reach hold in common. Employing the concepts explained earlier, marketing theory recognizes at least three aspects of participation: meeting needs, motivating clients to meet needs through the program in question, and informing clients of the program's availability.

Using these concepts to analyze lack of participation, a number of questions and issues are raised that have important programmatic implications. It seems axiomatic that the continuing education program should address client needs if participation is to be expected, but this axiom is often violated, which may be one reason for reluctance to participate.

Take, for example, the case of the Occupational Safety and Health Act (OSHA). When OSHA was enacted, it was realized that the new regulations would not be followed unless industrial personnel were aware of them. Thus, funds were made available to the extension division of a large university to hold a series of workshops outlining OSHA regulations. It soon became apparent that the industrial supervisors were not only reluctant to participate but, when they could be gathered together for a workshop, they also abandoned learning for the hotel bar at the earliest possible moment. In assessing the program's lack of success, extension staff quickly learned the reason. Although the federal government perceived a need for OSHA training, the participants did not. Quite to the contrary, they considered the topic to be irrelevant, boring, and demeaning.

Many programs designed for hard-to-reach populations are based on a societal need, rather than on needs perceived by the participant. A basic rationale for the Comprehensive Employment and Training Act (CETA) and the Adult Education Act legislation, for example, rests in manpower economics—the need for a high-quality, skilled workforce. When the intent of such legislation is translated to programs at the local level, there is no guarantee that the needs addressed will be perceived as needs by the populations targeted for participation.

Assuming that the continuing education agency has correctly assessed the needs of the hard-to-reach and has designed a program to meet them, information about the program must be conveyed to the hard-to-reach if they are to participate. In market analysis, it is important to ascertain the attributes of the hard-to-reach segment that might affect the dissemination of program information. This can present formidable problems, as typical methods of conveying information are frequently inappropriate for hard-to-reach populations.

Assuming that needs can be met and that an appropriate and effective medium is available for informing the hard-to-reach about the program, there still remains an important issue to confront in analyzing participation constraint. For any given set of needs, the likelihood exists that there are several options for dealing with them. If the need is not pressing, it can be ignored and frequently is. Clearly, there are often options other than education for coping with needs. Take, for example, non-English-speakers, for whom English as a Second Language (ESL) programming has been established. To cope, non-English-speakers can live in an ethnic ghetto where little English is spoken, they can learn English piecemeal from friends and from the television, or they can participate in formal ESL instruction. Living in an ethnic ghetto has the advantage of enabling the learner to cope without facing the formidable task of learning English. The obvious disadvantage is that, lacking the ability to speak English, the individual may find it difficult to function effectively in the larger society. Learning English informally through guided usage is a strategy that millions of immigrants have used successfully. The advantage is that time need not be taken away from normal activities to partake of formal instruction. The disadvantage is that to learn English thoroughly may take a longer period of time.

Like all adults, hard-to-reach adults generally have numerous options for meeting their needs. In fact, one reason why so many adults are hard to reach is that they tend to exercise options other than education for meeting their needs. The point is simply this: identifying a need of the hard-to-reach is necessary to secure participation but seldom sufficient. Once a need is identified, the client must be motivated to resolve it through the adult education program's services. Consequently, one of the most important things to be ascertained in market analysis is what is likely to motivate hard-to-reach clients to participate in educational programs.

After marketing segmentation has taken place and we have classified one or more hard-to-reach populations as groupings of clients to be served, there remain two more steps of market analysis to be conducted: consumer analysis, and analysis of competition.

Consumer Analysis. If there is any principle of program planning and evaluation that is firmly established in adult education, it is that learners' needs should be assessed before programs are established. Marketing recognizes this principle (Kotler, 1975) but goes several steps further by including program image assessment and satisfaction assessment as components of consumer analysis.

As Griffith (1978) implies, there may be a tendency among some adult educators to conceive of needs in a simplistic fashion and, as Monette (1977) points out, the concept of need itself is not at all clear. Suffice it to say here that consumer analysis recognizes at least two aspects of needs—overt needs and latent needs. Overt needs are needs the individual is aware of and can articulate relatively clearly. They are comparatively easy to assess, since, to acquire valid information, the educator need only query the respondent. The problem is that many of the most important needs of hard-to-reach adults do not operate on an overt level. Either the hard-to-reach adult is not aware of the need, has not sufficiently crystallized the need into a well-defined problem, or is not willing to articulate the need.

Perhaps nowhere is the distinction between overt and latent needs more pronounced than in the case of the elderly. The psychological research literature on the elderly portrays a vivid picture of the needs of older adults. The elderly tend to be relatively less happy, less self-confident, and to have less positive self-images (Kuhlen, 1969). They tend to withdraw emotional investments, give up self-assertiveness, avoid challenges, and generally turn inward, a process termed interiority (Rosen and Neugarten, 1964). Biological decline in later life restricts physical mobility and sensory input, thereby promoting social isolation, a condition frequently accentuated by loss of the spouse and the deaths of close friends.

It follows that, in dealing with the elderly, there is a need for interaction to combat social isolation, a need for catharsis to ameliorate interiority, and a need to enhance the ego by building self-esteem. Yet all these needs pertain to inner states of being and usually operate at the latent level. Generally speaking, the elderly cannot directly articulate such needs or have difficulty doing so.

An example of a needs assessment tapping the overt needs of the elderly is Hiemstra's (1975) work. When elderly respondents were asked to rank their preferences for thirty-two courses, four of the five highest-ranked course preferences related to instrumental needs such as "stretch your retirement dollar," "tax benefits for the older American," and "medical care in the retirement years" (p. 46). Thus, at the overt level, a very different needs constellation for older adults emerges, having to do with information for solving concrete, well-defined problems encountered by many older adults.

Certainly, an understanding of both needs dimensions is necessary in order to reach hard-to-reach groups. Overt needs can usually be effectively assessed through survey research or interview methods, providing that proper care is given to sample selection and instrument design. The assessment of latent needs may be more difficult. Promising approaches include literature searches, field-based research strategies such as grounded theory, and what Kotler (1975) calls "projective techniques" (p. 128). Among the projective techniques suggested are word association, sentence completion, picture completion, and role-playing. Kotler also suggests that simulation exercises may be useful in tapping latent needs (p. 129). Most of the techniques for assessing latent needs tend to be relatively subjective and require a measure of expertise in interpreting findings.

Even when we have correctly assessed the needs of our hard-to-reach population and have successfully translated those needs into relevant programs, participation is not ensured, for if the hard-to-reach adult is to participate, he or she must perceive that the continuing education program can and will meet his or her needs. Without this perception, the chances are that needs will be met elsewhere or not met at all. Analysis of this perception is part of image assessment.

As Mezirow, Darkenwald, and Knox (1975) suggest, public schools have an unfavorable image for many undereducated adults. Public schools are perceived to be child-oriented institutions. The school evokes unpleasant memories of confrontations with authority and failure in the classroom. To the extent that undereducated adults have unfavorable images of public schools and by association project those images on the public-school continuing education program, participation in public school-sponsored continuing education is unlikely. Consequently, if public-school continuing education programs wish to enroll hard-to-reach undereducated adults, they must understand the image many such adults hold of the schools.

Kotler suggests several techniques for assessing image, which he divides into two types—response methods and judgment methods. Response methods "do not prespecify any image attributes to the respondent. Rather, the respondent is asked to describe his image verbally or perform a task from which the image attributes will be inferred" (p. 132). Response methods, which are described in his book, include unstructured interviews, multidimensional scaling, and object sorting.

Judgment methods "specify image attributes in advance and ask respondents to rank, rate, or react to them" (Kotler, 1975, p. 132). Two common judgment methods are item lists, whereby respondents rate programs according to prespecified image attributes such as quality and prestige, and the semantic differential, in which respondents describe the program according to predetermined adjective pairs such as good-bad or expensive-inexpensive.

If image assessment indicates that the image the adult education agency wishes to project is not congruent with the image perceived by the hard-to-reach target population, efforts should be made to change the image through modifying price, place, product, promotion, or partners. If the image is positive, the program might still try to modify it to fit even more closely the favorable image held by potential participants. Conversely, if the image is negative, the program may try to change the perceptions of the hard-to-reach population. As Kotler (1975) cautions, many images are based on deep-seated values and attitudes and are thus difficult to change rapidly. It should also be remembered that image is but one of many factors that promote or impede reaching the hard-to-reach.

In addition to assessing needs and image, the state of satisfaction or demand should also be ascertained in consumer analysis. Demand refers to the degree to which the client wants the service rendered by the adult education program. The concept differs substantially from the concept of need. For example, while it may be assumed that chronic smokers, drug abusers, and obese persons need programs to remedy their problems, demand for such programming has been relatively slight. In fact, a suitable definition of "hard to reach" in marketing terms might be "any market segment for which the need for education surpasses the demand."

Although marketing specialists generally recognize at least eight states of demand—negative demand, no demand, latent demand, faltering demand, irregular demand, full demand, overfull demand, and unwholesome demand—the first three states are particularly important in respect to the hard-to-reach. A state of negative demand exists when clients are aware of the continuing education program but dislike it and may purposefully seek to avoid it. Participation is highly unlikely in the absence of strong external incentives or outright coercion. Mandatory safety classes for convicted motor vehicle offenders are an example of programming in the face of negative demand. There may be value as well as marketing issues associated with negative demand, for it may be impossible and unethical to teach the hard-to-reach something they do not wish to learn. Whether continuing professional education should be mandatory seems to be an example of conflict over value issues associated with negative demand.

In a no-demand situation, clients are indifferent; they neither desire the service nor seek to avoid it. Kotler (1975) notes three different no-demand situations. The first no-demand situation exists when familiar things or programs are perceived to be of no value to clients. The second situation exists when programs have value, but not in the specific market at hand. Finally, a no-demand situation exists when clients are simply unfamiliar with the program and therefore unaware of its value. While it is difficult to think of examples for the first situation, this is not the case for the other two. As Johnstone and Rivera (1965) note, disadvantaged adults often value education for its instrumental value, not for its own sake. Consequently, although there may be high demand for great-books and art appreciation courses among well-educated learners, there is little or no demand for such programs among the disadvantaged. Similarly, in respect to no-demand situations caused by lack of familiarity, failure to achieve widespread use of microfiche as an information dissemination medium may be attributed in part to the fact that many are unfamiliar with the medium and the use of microfiche readers. When a no-demand situation exists, stimulation marketing is warranted. As Kotler (1975) observes, there are three strategies. Programmers can attempt to connect the program with some existing need. For example, disadvantaged adults might be stimulated to enroll in art appreciation courses by gearing promotional activities to the felt need of parents to pass culture on to their children. The second strategy (Kotler, 1975) is to "alter the environment so that the offering becomes valued in the environment" (p. 83). If educational environments were altered so that microfiche readers were readily available, microfiche might become more highly valued and hence used by learners. The third strategy is to promote the program more vigorously, in hope that lack of demand is solely the result of lack of exposure.

A need for a program that does not exist is a latent-demand situation. Identifying and fulfilling latent demand is the major mission of program development. Clearly, a continuing education agency's ability to correctly assess and address latent demand is a key element of program success. In this regard, effective consumer analysis is obviously crucial. There are substantial rewards for the agency that taps latent demand, because there is little likelihood of substantial competition in the marketplace.

Lack of understanding about demand for continuing education may be one reason why there is difficulty in reaching hard-to-reach populations. Many programs for hard-to-reach populations are established to address social needs, rather than individual demand. Adult Basic Education, Cooperative Extension Urban Nutrition, and CETA training are examples of programs for hard-to-reach populations established in expectation that society would benefit as much as the individual. Yet all too often, when the objectives of these programs are translated into practice at the local level, there is minimal participation because a no-demand situation exists for the program as constituted by law or administrative mandate.

Analysis of Competition. After market segmentation and consumer analysis, the next step in market analysis is an assessment of the nature and extent of competition. The principle of competition recognizes that hard-to-reach adults typically have numerous options for meeting knowledge and skill needs. Each option is in competition with all others for gaining the hard-to-reach as users or clients. Those programs that understand the nature and form of such competition are in a better position to deal with it by providing service which is better than that of their competitors.

Kotler (1975, p. 59) notes four types of competition. Generic competition pertains to "broad product categories" that address the same client need. Let us assume that the hard-to-reach adult is young, chronically unemployed, and desires employment. Available options might include becoming an ACTION volunteer, relocating to a full-employment area of the country, or entering a CETA job skills program. From the perspective of the CETA program, education is competing with all other options for meeting the employment need. The fewer or more expensive the other options, the more likely is occupational education. If other options are extensive and inexpensive, the CETA program will have to provide better and less expensive service to gain clients. The second type of competition is product-form competition, competition among various forms of the same product. If the desired commodity is job skills, such skills might be gained through class attendance, on-the-job training, or self-study. Job skills taught in formal CETA programs are thus competing with these other forms of gaining job skills. Important attributes of the job skill product are the time it takes to gain proficiency, expense, and success at gaining desired employment. If other product forms are more favorable in respect to these attributes, the CETA program will find its clients difficult to reach.

Enterprise competition is the most commonly noted and refers to competition among programs and agencies that supply continuing education. A particular CETA program may be in competition with proprietary schools, vocational-technical schools, or community colleges in providing job skills. If the CETA program is to be successful in gaining hard-to-reach clients, it must achieve a mix of price, product, place, promotion, and partners that is more advantageous to the client than the mix of its competitors.

Although most continuing educators are well aware of enterprise competition in attempting to reach the hard-to-reach, many are less aware of product-form and generic competition as important concepts. Many hard-to-reach adults do meet their educational needs and do so quite effectively. As Tough's (1971) work suggests, however, they often rely on resources other than organized continuing education to do so.

Price, Product, Place, Promotion, and Partners

If marketing is to be successful in reaching the hard-to-reach, there should be two components to the marketing effort. Market analysis, which constitutes the first step, is basically an effort to gain important information about the market. The second step is to orchestrate program components on the basis of market analysis results. As suggested earlier, the purpose of such orchestration is to provide a program that optimizes participation by best satisfying client needs and demand. Although all aspects of a program should be so orchestrated, the most commonly discussed components from a marketing perspective are price, product, place, promotion, and partners.

Price. From a narrow perspective, price is defined as the amount of money charged by the continuing education agency for participation. Kotler (1975) discusses price setting in some detail and provides useful advice on the subject. In discussing the hard-to-reach, however, it is useful to conceptualize price more broadly than dollar cost charged. Thus conceived, price is the total value of all that is foregone in order to participate in continuing education. Clearly, dollar cost is a factor especially important for such traditionally hard-to-reach populations as the undereducated, the unemployed, and the elderly. Obviously, when less affluent populations are to be served, price should be set as low as possible. Yet even when fees are minimal, price can be quite high.

A very common price factor is time, specifically productive time that would otherwise be spent earning income. A case in point is a sales-oriented educational program offered to independent insurance agents by a large insurance company. As an incentive to participation, no fee was charged. Yet some agents were very difficult to reach despite the fact that the program had value for all. In fact, the most difficult to reach tended to be the most successful and affluent agents. Low demand undoubtedly affected lack of participation, because highly successful agents saw less of a need for education designed to bolster their effectiveness. Yet price was also an important factor. Successful agents considered every hour of their time to be so valuable that they were simply unwilling to pay the price of spending productive time on education. When time cost is a major marketing factor, educational activities should be organized in a fashion that minimizes time spent. Scheduling activities in close proximity to participants in order to reduce travel time and maximizing the efficiency of education to provide the greatest amount of learning per hour of instruction can help in this regard. Instructional technologies which enable learners to schedule their own time might also be considered.

Frequently, the price of attending continuing education includes hidden costs that can actually outweigh the fees charged. Transportation to learning activities, required instructional materials, and childcare are common hidden costs associated with hard-to-reach populations.

Product. The product of a continuing education program consists of everything it offers to the market for potential use, consumption, or adoption. In most cases the product would be a set of educational activities, though supportive services such as counseling or job placement may be part of the project as well. There are at least two ways in which product may be conceived. The most obvious is from the perspective of the tangible product defined by Kotler (1975) as "the physical entity or service that is offered to the target market" (p. 164). The tangible product of a continuing education program, for example, might be the courses, workshops, and conferences it offers. The second way to conceptualize product is from the perspective of the "augmented product," or the total meaning the product has for the user or potential user. Kotler notes that the augmented product includes the totality of benefits and costs involved in obtaining the product (p. 165).

Houle (1961) provides an interesting perspective on some of the benefits adults typically seek from continuing education. He notes that, while some adult learners participate in order to gain extrinsic benefits such as occupational advancement, others participate because they are "activity-oriented," and still others see intrinsic value in knowledge itself. Clearly, the degree to which a potential participant sees intrinsic, extrinsic, or other benefits from continuing education offerings will affect whether and how that product is used.

Conceptualizing the product from an augmented perspective is vital, for only in establishing the total meaning of the product from the consumer's perspective can the continuing education program gain an accurate understanding of the factors that motivate participation or lack of it. Although actual participation in continuing education occurs in relation to the tangible product, whether one participates and in what fashion has much more to do with the augmented product. If, to use a crude example, physicians view a continuing professional education workshop as an activity that will enhance their prestige and proficiency with little time cost, they may participate. If, however, the workshop is not seen as likely to enhance their prestige and proficiency, and if it involves substantial time costs, participation is unlikely.

If ability to reach the hard-to-reach is affected by product, there are essentially three marketing options: product addition, product modification, and product elimination. Products should be added or modified only after sound market analysis has provided information about desired product characteristics. Ideally, all new products should be field-tested on a limited basis before the entire program is committed to them.

Place. Several characteristics of place (the location of educational activities) have already been mentioned. It has been suggested that place often has a symbolic value affecting program image. Public schools may be symbols of failure for the undereducated, and universities may symbolize either prestige or academic snobbery. Place is affected by the situational variables mentioned in the first chapter, such as proximity to clients or accessibility to transportation. Kotler (1975) mentions three decisions that must be made in regard to place: level of service, quality of service, and number of delivery locations. Level of service refers to how much of a program's total service should be delivered per location. If we follow the well-established principle that, in serving hard-to-reach adults, location should be optimally accessible, the conclusion might be to operate from a number of sites where concentrations of the hard-to-reach are situated. Such a prescription is simplistic, however. If the number of sites is increased and the number of clients served per outlet is thus reduced, costs per client may rise substantially. In addition, logistical problems resulting in less effective coordination and quality-control may be incurred. Moreover, location dispersion may make it impossible to provide adequate supportive service. Take, for example, a current controversy in continuing professional education. Some cogently argue that more hard-to-reach clients will be reached if courses are conducted off campus, in the workplace and other places where clients are concentrated. Others argue that, in doing so, we reduce quality, for when courses are conducted off campus, participants have less access to such resources as libraries, laboratories, computers, or advisement. To provide these supportive services to widely dispersed off-campus locations could be prohibitively expensive. Similarly, we might maximize accessibility by conducting consumer education courses for the elderly in their own homes but, in so doing, we would sacrifice access to audiovisual aids and the benefits of group social interaction.

Promotion. Promotional efforts are consciously planned activities designed to communicate persuasively, to inform potential clients of the program, and to motivate participation. There are essentially five forms of promotion: advertising, publicity, personal contact, incentives, and atmospherics.

As defined by Kotler (1975), advertising "is any paid form of non-personal presentation and promotion of ideas, goods, or services by an identified sponsor" (p. 201). As a form of communication, an advertising message must be selected that is appropriate to the target audience. The message must be delivered through an appropriate channel with adequate frequency. Advertising efforts must be especially tailored and frequently repeated when dealing with hard-to-reach populations.

A defining characteristic of advertising is that it is paid for. Impersonal promotion which is not paid for is termed publicity. One of the best examples of program publicity was developed by the Cooperative Extension Service. In seeking adoption of new strains of corn and wheat, the Service asked selected farmers to plant a small section of the new strain next to their current crop. Such plantings were generally next to a highway where passersby could easily view the field. As the crop matured and the new planting was obviously healthier and of a higher yield than the farmer's current crop, adoption of the new strain by other farmers was easy to secure.

Publicity has several advantages over advertising. First, it costs little in comparison to advertising. Second, because it seldom appears so fabricated as advertising, publicity may have more credibility. Publicity may catch resistant clients off-guard and may have dramatic appeal if well orchestrated (Kotler, 1975).

Personal contact is a form of promotion that employs face-to-face interaction to inform and persuade. As Beder (1972) notes, ABE directors frequently were successful in establishing learner referral relationships with external agencies through face-to-face interaction at community meetings. Similarly, paid door-to-door recruiters have been effective in recruiting ABE students in some localities (Beder and Smith, 1977). Military recruiters "sell" training to potential enlistees, and Cooperative Extension Service county agents spend much of their time in face-to-face promotional efforts. Although advertising and promotion can generally reach larger numbers of people at less expense per person contacted, more complex messages can be communicated through personal contact. Moreover, a two-way communication process is involved that allows the program representative to adjust the message in response to the recipient's feedback.

Kotler (1975) defines incentives as "something of financial value added to an offer to encourage some overt behavioral response" (p. 217). Granting cash stipends to CETA trainees is an example of an incentive. Atmospherics—altering the setting or ambiance of continuing education to make it more appealing to participants—is another promotional strategy. Many professional conference centers have been quite successful in using atmospherics as promotional tools. Rich paneling, soft music, and lush carpets may give an atmosphere of prestige or importance to the educational activity. Arrangement of seating may help create an atmosphere that can range from businesslike austerity to friendly informality. A drawback to atmospherics as a promotional tool is that the client may have to have encountered the setting before the promotional effect registers. This may be difficult to achieve for many hard-to-reach groups.

Partners. Partners, defined as the purposeful establishment of interorganizational relationships to facilitate agency goal attainment, has two major dimensions in respect to hard-to-reach populations (Lauffler, 1977). The first we shall term participation; the second, service.

One of the most promising and cost-effective strategies for securing participation of hard-to-reach populations is simply to work closely with other organizations and agencies that have been successful in reaching them. There are two common relationships in this regard—cosponsorship and referral. In a cosponsorship relationship, the continuing education agency and an organization that serves the hard-to-reach cooperate to provide a joint program. In referral, other agencies refer their clients to continuing education. As a result, the continuing education agency gains preferential access to a pool of hard-to-reach learners, while cooperating organizations and agencies gain access to education for their clients. The basis for the relationship, then, is reciprocity—all partners to the relationship benefit by cooperation. Beder and Smith (1977) note than an urban ABE program was successful in reaching large groups of unemployed adults by establishing a referral relationship with the employment service. By referring to the ABE program clients who were unemployable because of low literacy skills, the employment service could claim it benefited clients whom it could not have helped otherwise. The ABE program benefitted from the large number of clients sent to it and by the fact that ABE graduates could in turn be sent back to the employment service for jobs. Hence the ABE program gained job placement capability as a second benefit.

Just as the partners concept can affect access to hard-to-reach groups, it can also promote better service. For many hard-to-reach populations, continuing education is necessary but not sufficient for achieving ultimate objectives. Continuing education is but one step in getting a job, maintaining good health, becoming a more effective parent, and so forth. Putting all the steps together into a viable strategy can be so complex and difficult that the ultimate objectives are simply abandoned. If, through cooperative interorganizational efforts, a wide range of coordinated services can be afforded the client, not only do the cooperating partners benefit but so, too, does the client.

The marketing approach is one effective strategy for reaching hard-to-reach adults. Let us highlight the elements of the approach that promote its effectiveness. The first element is the notion of differential response. Clients volunteer to participate in continuing education because the program fulfills a want, desire, or need. Clients participate because they receive value from doing so, value which exceeds all costs associated with participation. Yet value and cost vary greatly for different client groups. Consequently, differential response requires that the potential market for continuing education be segmented, or grouped according to what the market segments value, as well as to the costs they incur in participating. The program then responds to each market segment in a fashion particularly appropriate to that segment. The implication for reaching hard-to-reach adults is that, rather than considering the hard-to-reach to be incorrigible nonparticipants, continuing educators consider such populations to be special market segments to which special responses must be made to secure participation. In marketing, reaching the hard-to-reach is a problem to be solved, rather than a cause for despair.

The second element is holism. In marketing, all program components are variables to be manipulated in the interest of client satisfaction. The marketing approach is highly client-centered, rather than program-centered. This differs markedly from other approaches, which assume that the program is a given that is subsequently publicized in expectation that participation will result. In such cases, those who do not participate are termed "hard to reach." In the marketing approach, the highly integrated components of product, price, promotion, place, and partners are orchestrated to appeal to all high-priority market segments. In combination with differential response, the holistic concept promotes participation of the hard-to-reach, simply because the program thereby provides better service to them.

Although providing maximum value to the client is the central element of marketing, value alone is often insufficient for securing participation. This leads to the third element — persuasive communication. In continuing education, actual value generally has to be experienced; it is not obtained until participation has actually occurred. Consequently, advance notice of potential value must be communicated in a way that effectively motivates initial efforts to participate. This is a vital principle if we assume that many hard-to-reach populations fail to participate primarily because they are unaware of the value to be gained through continuing education.

The final element of effectiveness is proved technique. Many approaches to programming in continuing education operate only at the theoretical-conceptual level. Their sole utility lies in helping us to understand programming and organize that understanding. Other so-called approaches are merely collections of unrelated techniques. Although they may provide useful information on how to develop programs, they entail neither theoretical rationales for doing so nor understanding regarding why a given technique is likely to succeed or to fail. Marketing, however, includes both theoretical-conceptual and proved practical application components. That is one more reason why the marketing approach has special utility for those who wish to reach hard-to-reach adults for continuing education.

References

Beder, H. W. "Community Linkages in Urban Public School Adult Basic Education Programs: A Study of Cosponsorship and the Use of Community Liaison Personnel." Unpublished doctoral dissertation, Teachers College, Columbia University, 1972.

Beder, H. W., and Smith, F. B. *Developing an Adult Education Program through Community Linkages.* Washington, D.C.: Adult Education Association, 1977.

Griffith, W. S. "Educational Needs: Definition, Assessment, and Utilization." *School Review,* 1978, *86* (3), 382–394.

Hiemstra, R. *The Older Adult and Learning.* Ames: Iowa State University, 1975.

Houle, C. *The Inquiring Mind.* Madison: University of Wisconsin Press, 1961.

Johnstone, W., and Rivera, R. *Volunteers for Learning.* Chicago: Aldine, 1965.

Kotler, P. *Marketing for Nonprofit Organizations*. Englewood Cliffs, N.J.: Prentice-Hall, 1975.

Kuhlen, R. G. "Developmental Changes in Motivation During the Adult Years." In J. E. Birren (Ed.), *Relations of Development and Aging*. Springfield, Ill.: Charles C. Thomas, 1969.

Lauffler, A. *The Practice of Continuing Education in the Human Services*. New York: McGraw-Hill, 1977.

Mezirow, J., Darkenwald, G., and Knox, A. *Last Gamble on Education*. Washington, D.C.: Adult Education Association, 1975.

Monette, M. L. "The Concept of Educational Need: An Analysis of Selected Literature." *Adult Education*, 1977, 27, 116–127.

Rosen, J. L., and Neugarten, B. L. "Ego Functions in the Middle and Late Years: A Thematic Apperception Study." In B. L. Neugarten (Ed.), *Personality in Middle and Late Life*. New York: Atherton Press, 1964.

Tough, A. *The Adult's Learning Projects*. Toronto: The Ontario Institute for Studies in Education, 1971.

Harold W. Beder is associate professor of adult and continuing education and codirector, Center for Adult Development, Graduate School of Education, Rutgers University. A past chairman of the Adult Education Association's Commission on Research and a consulting editor of Adult Education, *he has written extensively in the area of program development and evaluation.*

Reaching the hard-to-reach is ultimately a matter of communication. As viewed here, communication is a means of motivating participation and providing new methods of instruction.

Overcoming Barriers to Communication

Gordon A. Larson

Communication is an essential part of any educational activity, but within the field of continuing education it plays an even greater role than in the more traditional public school and higher education systems. In the public school sector, the study of communications is focused primarily on increasing the efficacy of classroom teaching, with a secondary interest in the use of electronic systems for administrative uses. Higher education is concerned with two additional uses of communications. To a greater extent than in previous eras, colleges and universities today use communications as part of a marketing strategy to attract students in what is becoming a buyer's market in education. A second major use of communications in higher education is in providing linkages between institutions to facilitate the dissemination and transfer of knowledge. This role is particularly evident in the use of computer technology such as the PLATO system, which links members of the research community and progressive members of the instructional community in a worldwide network. Another manifestation of this linkage system is the complex communications networks established between components of a widespread higher education system (Chamberlain, 1980.)

  Continuing education has a more difficult role of providing a wide variety of educational services to a more heterogeneous target population than those served by the public schools and resident instruction programs of higher education. While media techniques developed by commercial or political interests to reach the greatest percentage of the general population at the least cost may suit the educational purposes of traditional learning systems, the problem of reaching hard-to-reach adults through continuing education has resisted easy solutions by conventional mass-media techniques.

Purposes of Communications

Communications serve two general purposes in continuing education. The first is to attract adults to existing educational programs conducted by continuing education providers. This is the promotional aspect of marketing strategies discussed in the previous chapter. The second general purpose of communications is to transmit knowledge and information directly to the target population. While this second purpose applies to all instructional processes, we are concerned here primarily with the dissemination of education over distance through employment of modern communications technology (Chamberlain, 1980). These two purposes of communications illustrate two major strategies for reaching hard-to-reach populations. The promotional strategy is based on an assumption that low participation results from lack of information or motivation and that success will be gained by pointing out the advantages of participation and informing the target audience of the availability and location of existing services. Emphasis in this approach is on broad distribution of the message and persuasive content.

The second strategy might be called the outreach approach. It assumes that participation among hard-to-reach populations is inhibited primarily by problems in availability of educational services, and that electronic media can be used to provide educational programs to these populations at convenient locations, as George Eyster observed about educational television (ETV), "ETV has the capability of reaching into virtually every home, school, and building in America—the greatest potential of reaching the greatest number of unserved adults in their homes or wherever they are. ETV can serve and reach those people who (1) cannot or will not participate in formal programs; (2) are home-, job-, or family-bound; (3) are fearful of failure, and other people; or (4) are reluctant to admit publicly not having a high school diploma" (1976, p. 109). However, Eyster notes that educational television has not lived up to its promise, due to failure on the part of educators to employ it properly. Part of the problem is that educators have lacked a sound research basis for meeting the needs of the hard-to-reach. Advice provided to the educational practitioner in the literature has normally consisted of how to adapt commercial communication techniques to the general educational process with little or no consideration given to addressing special problems associated with communicating to hard-to-reach populations.

The Communications Process

Several complex models, which would be impossible to deal with adequately in this chapter, have been advanced to explain the communications process. At the most basic level, communcation may be viewed as a one-way process consisting of six elements: a source (who) transmits a message (what) for some purpose (why) by some channel or medium (how) to a user (to whom) with some effect (Havelock, 1971). At a slightly more complex level, this process could involve a series of communications from an original source through a series of intermediate linkages to the ultimate user with feedback systems operating at each linkage. Each linking unit or person acts as both a receiver and transmitter of the message, and each may modify the message slightly, as has been often demonstrated in parlor games. Even when the message is direct from the source to the user, the message may not serve its intended purpose, as a result of one or any combination of intrapersonal, interpersonal, technical, or sociological barriers to the communications process. As Havelock (1971) notes, these barriers have a filtering or screening effect on the message, allowing selected parts of the message or messages to go through while other parts are stopped. These barriers could exist at the source, as a factor of the medium of transmission, or at the receiver level.

Some of the factors that influence the fidelity of message transmission and reception include role perceptions of the source and the user; status discrepancies or ambiguities, such as age or race; language differences (including cultural or dialectic nuances); and timing of the message. In the following sections we will consider two major factors in the communication process that have significant impact on reaching the hard-to-reach — communications technology and psychosocial variables associated with cultural differences.

Communications Technology

The current rapid growth of technology in communications has created unprecedented potential for delivery of educational programming, limited only by the educator's imagination and, to a much lesser extent, by current costs of the electronic systems. In the past decade, cassette tape recorders, videotape recorders, computers, cable television, and communications satellites have altered traditional means of disseminating knowledge (Chamberlain, 1980). A recently developed system known as videodisk may provide a more cost-effective home-deliv-

ery system for education and entertainment than is available from previous systems. Videodisk systems use audiovisual recordings similar to
a phonograph record that can be played into a regular television set
and stereo system. The major advantage of this system for education is
that the videodisks can be produced in greater quantity and at a lower
cost than videotapes, thus facilitating mass-marketing of audiovisual
educational programs.

Great potential impact on educational delivery systems can be
expected from the combination of computers, communications satellites, telephones, videodisks, and cable television into home-based information systems that can be used to meet several different educational
needs. Videotext and teletext systems already available may be linked
to libraries and information systems to bring books and articles into the
home electronically. Two-way cable television systems such as Qube will
allow students to order specific home-study courses, pay for them through
a built-in credit card system, and engage in dialogue with the instructor
through a computerized link with the continuing educator. With a two-
way cable television system, teachers will be able to conduct continuing
education classes from long distances, and educators will be able to
conduct continuing education seminars for professionals without having them travel away from their jobs. From a purely technological standpoint, the potential for delivery of continuing education services appears
unlimited, but before we embrace improved technology as a panacea
for all of our educational ills, we should consider the experience of educational television.

Effects of Technology

King (1979) cites a 1961 statement by J. C. Poolock, extolling
the virtues of television learning and calling it the "greatest opportunity
for the advancement of education since the introduction of printing by
movable type" (p. 4). She notes that "after a decade of intensive effort
and the expenditure of hundreds of millions of dollars, television has
not made a decisive impact on schools and colleges in this country."
Eyster (1976) concurs in this lackluster assessment of the impact of educational television, and results of other studies show that television has
failed to reach the disadvantaged populations to the degree expected.

Why has educational television failed to live up to its promise?
King (1979) attributes the failure to educators' neglect of their own
research on adult learning. She cites evidence to show that television
can be an effective educational tool when properly employed. She suggests that greater success would have been achieved if educators made
provisions for active participation of learners in the process, if they
packaged programs into smaller self-contained modules, if they pro-

vided for feedback and self-pacing, and if programs were related to immediate needs of the adult students. If these conjectures are valid, the developments described earlier in this section will improve the potential of educational technology in the hands of creative continuing educators to reach more difficult target audiences. King suggests that educators must have greater awareness of cross-cultural impacts of face-to-face relationships and body kinetics in designing software for minority populations. She also suggests that adults deficient in basic education require more personal contact and reassurance than the average consumer of educational TV. This assertion is supported by other research.

Eyster (1976) claims that educational television has produced high-quality, interesting instruction, but notes that its impact on adult achievement has been disappointing. He also asserts that educational television is as effective as any other method of instruction, and that lack of success has been due to failures to provide adequate support systems for the students, rather than problems in technology or software design. He notes that "even the most nominal person-to-person contact is the critical element in the successful utilization of ETV on open broadcast—critical to student involvement, student retention, student perseverance, and student achievement" (p. 110).

This assertion is supported by Robinson (1979), who cites evidence to suggest that, without cooperating agencies, educational broadcasting cannot provide the needed range of learning opportunities. He sees the need for these agencies to provide diagnostic and assessment services, course development, distribution of materials, enrollment and tuition services, counseling, tutoring, accreditation, student assessment, evaluation, and funding. He cites the example of the Open University, which was unsuccessful at meeting learning needs of adults through television and radio courses until it established cooperative support systems through local education agencies. A more relevant example for hard-to-reach populations cited by Robinson was the BBC series for illiterate adults, "On the Move." It was designed not as an instructional intervention but primarily as a promotion vehicle to reach people with major reading and writing difficulties in their own homes and to reassure them that they could benefit from formal instruction. Television programs were short and lively and included a segment in which a nonreader reported progress made in reading, a motivational technique similar to that employed by Alcoholics Anonymous. The programs provided the viewer with information needed to contact a local education agency for conduct of the actual instruction. Through this process, the BBC has enrolled more than 100,000 illiterate adults in reading programs.

An interesting aspect of this example is that it achieved success through combining the instructional and promotional potential of the media. It also illustrates that technology alone is not enough to satisfy all the needs of hard-to-reach student populations. This may be explained both in terms of research on learning described earlier and by the research on participation motivation (Boshier, 1977). Of the six motivational factors identified by Boshier, at least two cannot be satisfied by mass media alone. Both the need for social contact and the need for escape/stimulation are best satisfied by group-oriented activities outside the home. Boshier found that these two factors, while not decisive by themselves, were often secondary influences on participation. Given the delicate balance between participation and nonparticipation among the hard-to-reach, these motivational factors cannot be overlooked.

The Gap Effect

In addition to the psychological barriers that inhibit use of technology, research on communication in foreign cultures has suggested that use of mass media and standard dissemination techniques widens the knowledge gap between the "haves" and the "have nots" (Roling, Ascroft, and Chege, 1976; Shingi and Mody, 1976). Shingi and Mody explain that gaps may occur because new information is provided at a rate and in a format that exceed the capacity of lower SES groups to absorb and assimilate the materials. The more progressive and advanced elements of society have better communications skills; more accumulated information; a wider range of relevant social contacts; and greater potential for selective exposure, acceptance, and retention of the information. Thus, as the flow of information is increased by mass media, the "haves" absorb the information more rapidly and put it to more effective use than the "have nots." Shingi and Mody found that this was not always the case, however. When information contains a high percentage of facts already included in the knowledge base of the "haves," a ceiling effect limits the amount of learning that takes place for this group. The "have nots" are able to use more of the information provided in the message, and are thus able to close the gap. The major variable accounting for relative gains appears to be knowledge of technical terms. When familiarity with technical vocabulary is assumed by the communicator and no explanations are offered in the message, the knowledge gap is likely to widen. Conversely, if a large portion of the message is devoted to explaining technical terminology, the ceiling effect occurs and one can expect the gap to close. This is an important consideration when planning instruction for the educationally disadvantaged.

Intrapersonal Barriers

Intrapersonal barriers to communication result from conflicts between the content or purpose of the message and various personality traits of the individual. We have limited the discussion to a group of traits identified by Havelock (1971) that tend to facilitate or impede attempts to influence individuals in the communication process. Members of certain hard-to-reach groups have a greater number of traits that negatively influence the communications process, and educators must be aware of these factors and make efforts to circumvent or overcome them.

Negative sense of competence and self-esteem is a major inhibiting factor in reaching disadvantaged adult populations. The individual who feels less competent is less receptive to suggestions that will require involvement in new ventures such as education. As noted in an earlier section, some success has been achieved in overcoming this problem by use of confidence-building media-based programs, coupled with an effective personal support system of counseling and interpersonal contacts.

A second factor noted by Havelock is the authoritarian personality and its related trait of dogmatism. These traits are the root of prejudice and cause the individual to reject attempts to be influenced by outside sources. One method for dealing with this problem is to use change agents selected from within the target population.

Values are strongly held beliefs that influence the degree to which an individual will accept or reject a message. Acceptance depends on the extent to which an individual perceives the purpose of the message to be congruent with his or her own values. Havelock suggests six strategies for coping with individual values. They include emphasizing values congruent with the communicator's purpose, bypassing value issues, negotiating value issues, exposing value issues to logical scrutiny, appealing to key values in message design, and respecting values as barriers. Successful strategies depend on correct identification of the dominant values in the individual and selection of the course of action most appropriate to the particular relationship existing between purpose and values.

Another psychological characteristic that is well recognized by continuing educators is the concept of need. We are advised to conduct a needs assessment as part of the educational planning process. What is not always recognized is that needs identified and valued by society may not be felt by the individual. If this is the case, these needs have no motivational effect. A case in point is the provision of literacy instruction to individuals whom society has defined as functional illiterates. If individuals so identified do not perceive that they have serious literacy dysfunctions, they will be unlikely to participate. One of the purposes of communications might be to convince the individual that the need exists.

Past experience is an individual characteristic that predisposes people to act in certain established patterns. This inertial tendency is called set. An obvious characteristic of hard-to-reach adult populations is that they are predisposed to avoid participation in education. This tendency is exacerbated by the fact that new information is less likely to have an effect if the individual has already been exposed to large amounts of information on the subject. It may be anticipated, therefore, that hard-to-reach adults are likely to have built up a resistance to efforts to persuade them to participate.

Fear and anxiety have a strong influence on acceptance of ideas. However, the use of threats or appeals to fear for purposes of persuasion may have the opposite effect to that intended. This has been shown in attempts to persuade people to quit smoking. Appeals based on the danger of cancer have caused high-anxiety situations in which individuals seek out other smokers for support, reinforcing their smoking habit.

Interpersonal Barriers

While intrapersonal barriers result from conflicts between the message and the intended recipient, interpersonal barriers result from conflicting relationships between the two individuals doing the communicating. There are many interpersonal factors which may operate for or against effective communication. Havelock (1971) has identifed four of the most important, which illustrate the problem.

Role-perception and definition conflicts exist when either the "resources" or the "users" do not understand or accept their respective roles. In reaching hard-to-reach populations, the intended recipient of a message may not admit the need for outside help or may not accept the individual who is transmitting the message as an appropriate source of information. In either case, unless both the resource and the user are persuaded to accept their roles, it is unlikely that efforts to transmit needed information will be effective.

A related source of interpersonal conflict is status discrepancy or ambiguity. Havelock notes that effective communication is unlikely to occur if the recipients feel that by engaging in communications with the source their status will be threatened. This perception of threat is likely to occur when a perceived status discrepancy exists between the source of the message and the intended user of the message. Age, sex, and racial differences may create unacceptable status discrepancies among many hard-to-reach populations. Older adults may find it threatening to accept information from younger adults, men may find it difficult to take advice from women, and persons of one race may feel threatened accepting advice from a person of another race. These perceived differences are prejudicial and undesirable, but if we fail to take them into account in our communications strategies, we may encounter difficulties in reaching our target audiences.

Language or dialect is another potential barrier in the communication process. This is so obvious that at first consideration it seems hardly worth mentioning. While we all recognize the need to communicate in the language of the target population, we often overlook subtle differences in dialect and jargon. Politicians have been known to use different accents and dialects when dealing with certain elements of their constituencies than they use in conversation with people from other parts of the country. This is equally true of other prominent figures who must maintain credibility in more than one subculture. While these linguistic transformations may be affected for purely cosmetic purposes, they also serve to facilitate communications. Many words and phrases undergo subtle transformations in meaning among various subcultures which speak the same basic language. To achieve maximum effect, messages should be transmitted in the dialect or encoding scheme shared between the sender and receiver.

A fourth factor affecting the receptivity of an interpersonal com- ·munication is the timing of the message. Havelock refers to this effect as being out of phase. The communicator creates a high probability of failure by attempting to transmit a message at a time when the receiver is not prepared or not interested in receiving it. An obvious example of this would be broadcasting information on how to receive help in preparing income tax forms on April 16th. A less apparent, but perhaps more plausible, example of this phenomenon is the case of a teacher who has an innovative idea for improving instruction in the school. The teacher brings the new idea to the attention of the principal when he or she is in the middle of budget negotiations with the school board. At that moment, the principal is not receptive to an idea that would have been well received at another time. Obviously, communications strategies should attempt to identify the "reachable moment" and time messages accordingly.

Educators must take into consideration the interpersonal factors of role, status, language, and timing when attempting to communicate with hard-to-reach groups. They should also be aware of intrapersonal traits that increase or decrease the receptivity of the individual in planning content and choosing media. Each of the factors mentioned so far operates at an individual level and the combination of factors is different for each person. Given the limited resources available to continuing education agencies, it would seem impossible to provide the kind of personal consideration that would account for all of these individual factors. Fortunately, as Havelock (1971) and Rogers and Shoemaker (1971) have noted, social groups have a unifying influence over the responsiveness of their members to new ideas. We may be able to achieve success in overcoming barriers at the individual level by understanding and taking advantage of group dynamics in the communications process.

Group Influences

Social groups may be large or small and have varying degrees of organizational structure and cohesiveness. These properties affect the degree of influence that the group has over its members. Formal organizations have both formal and informal means of influencing members, while informal social organizations rely mostly on informal group pressures to achieve individual conformity. Small groups are likely to exert tighter control over their members than do large groups. Most hard-to-reach populations can be identified only as large, informal, and minimally cohesive groups constituting major subcultures of society, such as disadvantaged Blacks or Hispanics, the aged, or rural dwellers. Other hard-to-reach adults are members of formal organizations such as the medical or legal professions. The principles and processes discussed in this section apply to both types of groups, but to varying degrees.

All groups have identities based on shared characteristics of their members. To the extent that individuals wish to identify with a given group, they must accept and abide by certain expected behavior patterns, which are based on shared values and are called norms. Norms may be stated explicitly in some form of ethical code such as the Hippocratic oath or they may be unstated group expectations arrived at through custom and tradition. Violation of group norms is usually punished by some type of formal or informal group sanction. An example of formal sanction would be disbarment from the legal profession, while an example of informal sanction is the practice of "binging" (punching a coworker on the arm in order to gain compliance to the working group's standards and norms) overly ambitious "rate busters," which was observed in the Hawthorne plant studies in the thirties.

Within groups, certain individuals exert more influence over the establishment of norms and have greater freedom in violating norms than others. They are called opinion leaders. Rogers and Shoemaker (1971) note that opinion leaders tend to be more cosmopolitan, more exposed to external communications, and more innovative than followers. Their degree of innovativeness varies, depending upon whether the group is traditional or modern. Rogers and Shoemaker define traditional groups as those which exhibit conservative characteristics such as lack of favorable orientation to change, less well-developed technology, low levels of education and literacy, and rigid maintenance of traditional social values. Modern groups, in contrast, exhibit more innovative tendencies. Opinion leaders tend to reflect the basic orientation of their groups, but are slightly ahead of their groups in accepting new ideas.

Two effective ways of influencing group acceptance of a message are by involving the group in the decision-making process and by persuading the opinion leaders, who in turn influence their group. The most extreme proponent of the group decision-making process in education is Paulo Freire (1973), who advocates that educators should raise people's self-awareness to the point where they will establish their own goals and devise their own means of obtaining those goals. Many educators would find themselves uncomfortable allowing that much latitude in program direction and would prefer that potential clients participate only in an advisory capacity. One way of doing this is to form an advisory group of opinion leaders from the target population. They can advise on program goals and methods and, having accepted these goals, they can advise on how to communicate them to potential participants or can serve as a direct interpersonal link with the target population.

In selecting opinion leaders, educators must be careful that they do not identify the wrong people. In this regard, two common sources of error should be avoided. The first common error is to choose someone based only on formal status in the group. Often persons in formal authority positions lack the informal power to influence group opinion. The real opinion leaders may avoid positions of formal power in order to retain their identification as members of the group. The second common error is to select someone from the group because that person is highly receptive to the proposed idea or change. The most innovative members of the group often have low status within the group due to their frequent departure from normative standards.

Cultural Factors

A concept which is closely related to group norms is that of culture. Culture is a system of values and norms shared by members of an ethnic group by virtue of their common heritage. Education, whether conducted formally or informally, is the primary means by which a society transmits cultural values from one generation to the next. One of the factors that has contributed to our failure to reach certain populations has been a failure to recognize or tolerate the values and norms of minority cultures in our society. In the past, most of our educative systems have been based on a melting-pot theory, which required that all members of minority cultures be assimilated into one dominant American culture. Recent research and theory have suggested that Hispanic and Native American ethnic groups have rejected assimilation as the avenue to success in American society, and that this has contributed significantly to their lack of achievement and participation in formal education programs (Glass and Goulding, 1977; Paulston, 1976; Vela, 1977). What was once perceived as a language problem is now perceived as a cultural barrier. In attempting to reach members of minority subcultures, educators must consider the perceived implications of their proposals among the cultural minority. Programs that are perceived as threats to cultural identity will be rejected. In order to obviate these fears of cultural obliteration, multicultural approaches to instructional design and communications should be adopted.

References

Boshier, R. "Motivational Orientations Revisited: Life-Space Motives and the Education Participation Scale." *Adult Education,* 1977, *27* (2), 89–115.

Chamberlain, M. (Ed.). *New Directions for Continuing Education: Providing Continuing Education by Media and Technology,* no. 5. San Francisco: Jossey-Bass, 1980.

Eyster, G. W. "ETV Utilization in Adult Education." *Adult Leadership,* 1976, *25* (4), 109–110.

Freire, P. *Education for Critical Consciousness.* New York: Seabury Press, 1973.

Glass, J. C., and Goulding, L. J. "The Mexican-American and Adult Education." *Adult Leadership,* 1977, *25* (6), 185–190.

Havelock, R. G. *Planning for Innovation Through Dissemination and Utilization of Knowledge.* Ann Arbor, Mich.: Center for Research on Utilization of Scientific Knowledge, 1971.

King, L. R. "The Effective Use of Television in Adult Education." *Lifelong Learning,* 1979, *2* (7), 4–7.

Johnson, E. I. *Metroplex Assembly.* Research Report, Center for the Study of Liberal Education for Adults. Syracuse, N.Y.: Publications in Continuing Education, Syracuse University, 1965.

Paulston, C. B. "Ethnic Relations and Bilingual Education: Accounting for Contradictory Data." In J. E. Alatis and K. Twaddel (Eds.), *English as a Second Language in Bilingual Education.* Washington, D.C.: TESOL, 1976.

Robinson, J. "Educational Broadcasting and Socially Deprived Groups in the Adult Community." *Adult Education* (British), 1979, *51* (6), 337–344.

Rogers, E. M. (Ed.). *Communication and Development: Critical Perspectives.* Beverly Hills, Calif.: Sage, 1976.

Rogers, E. M., and Shoemaker, F. *Communication of Innovations.* New York: Free Press, 1971.

Roling, N. G., Ascroft, J., and Chege, F. W. "The Diffusion of Innovations and the Issue of Equity in Rural Development." In E. M. Rogers (Ed.), *Communication and Development: Critical Perspectives.* Beverly Hills, Calif.: Sage, 1976.

Shingi, P. M., and Mody, B. "The Communications Gap: A Field Experiment on Television and Agricultural Ignorance in India." In E. M. Rogers (Ed.), *Communication and Development: Critical Perspectives.* Beverly Hills, Calif.: Sage, 1976.

Vela, J. E. "The Mexican-American in Adult Education: A Reaction." *Adult Leadership,* 1977, *25* (8), 246–247.

Gordon A. Larson is assistant professor of adult education and reading and codirector, Center for Adult Development, Graduate School of Education, Rutgers University.

Only 2.2 percent of the least educated and lowest-income adults
participate in educational programs, yet these programs may
offer the best hope for upgrading their earning power
and integrating them into productive social and
economic roles in the community.

Reaching the Least
Educated Adult

Gladys H. Irish

Data compiled by the National Advisory Council on Adult Education
(*Adult Education . . .* , 1971, p. 21) indicate that only 4.25 percent of
adults without a high school diploma participated in basic education or
high school completion programs during fiscal year 1976. In round numbers, only 3.3 million adults enrolled in these programs, although in
total some 65 million adults lack a high school diploma.

The adults who are most underserved are those who not only
lack a high school diploma but also are young (seventeen to twenty-
five), are in the lowest quarter of annual family income, and are members of minority racial groups (Anderson and Darkenwald, 1979). A
national probability sample survey indicated that in 1975 only 2.2 percent of those adults in the lowest quarter of family income and lacking a
high school diploma participated in educational programs. This same
survey indicated that only 1.3 percent of adults with less than a high
school education were enrolled in basic education or high school completion programs (Anderson and Darkenwald, 1979).

A survey of adult basic education program directors conducted
in 1973 found that almost 80 percent of the directors felt that improved
recruitment strategies were of critical importance to improving adult
basic education programs and half indicated that this was the most
important area for improvement (Mezirow and Irish, 1974, p. 9). The

problem was stated succinctly by continuing educators in Iowa: "Since adult basic education programs have been in existence for some time, it has become clear that those who were waiting for the opportunity for further education have been served. . . . Now the question has arisen as to how to reach the indifferent and resistant undereducated" (Iowa State Department of Instruction, 1974, pp. 39–40).

Barriers

Much attention has been given to delineating the general characteristics of the so-called "disadvantaged." While these will be reviewed in this section from the perspective of how they may create barriers to participation, it should be emphasized that actual as well as perceived efficacy of educational programs in enhancing the quality of participants' lives is an important influence on participation. For this reason, not only recruitment strategies but also programming innovations will be discussed. Where economic conditions are such that potential participants in educational upgrading programs have little or no expectation of eventually holding decent jobs, even programming changes may do little to enhance program attractiveness unless they incorporate some commitment to community change.

Least educated adults share with other adult learners distinctive characteristics that affect their participation in learning activities. These characteristics, however, may emerge in specific forms that are particularly foreign to the common assumptions and approaches of formal educational settings. One assumption is that adult learners have definite goals and objectives. The least educated have few goals that are dependent upon educational achievement simply because they do not believe such goals are within reach. All adults have distinct abilities and aptitudes. In the case of the least educated these may include complex strategies to compensate for their lack of reading and computational skills as well as for coping with daily problems and bureaucratic demands that do not confront most literate adults. These abilities and aptitudes are seldom recognized within the formal educational setting, let alone reflected in the learning process. While the least educated adult may have a great deal of knowledge in a particular area and be a respected member of his or her community, members of the educational system often fail to recognize this proficiency and these skills or to acknowledge their value. Adults are voluntary learners, who need to have their self-esteem and self-worth reinforced within the educational setting. While educators recognize the need for positive reinforcement and for creating success experiences for adult learners, the least educated often receive less of this positive support within the educational environment. Adult learners expect new learning to be relevant to their life experiences and to specific and concrete tasks they face in the community, family, and work settings.

The least educated adults may, in many instances, have experienced chronic failure in school. For this reason, they may be fearful about returning to that setting. Lack of self-confidence and low self-esteem, coupled with low verbal facility and the low perceived value of education commonly create high barriers to participation. Each of these must be combatted if the least educated are to enroll in educational activities. Researchers have also identified other psychological attributes which are commonly found among adults who have had life histories characterized by low income, minority group status, and limited options in areas such as work, housing, food, and health care. These include insecurity, distrust, fatalism, low aspirations, limited time perspective, dependency, localism, and lack of empathy (Anderson and Niemi, 1970). Adults with such attitudes cannot be expected to make the decision to participate in adult education activities without a great deal of encouragement and support.

Several model projects will be described that have been successful in reaching out to this group, and information will be given concerning how to effectively use each of three strategies to recruit this group: mass media, referrals, and direct personal recruitment. The chapter will conclude by noting several programming innovations with potential for enhancing initial and sustained participation by the least educated, most in need adult (*Catalog . . . ,* 1978, 1979).

Three Model Projects

The three projects discussed here are: REACH, the Adult Armchair Education Project, and POR-FIN. They operated in different parts of the country: South Bend, Philadelphia, and San Antonio. Although each had a different approach, together they demonstrate how best to reach out to the least educated adult.

REACH. Project REACH was a two-year special experimental demonstration project conducted by the University of Notre Dame for the purpose of finding new and economical means of increasing enrollment in adult basic education programs. Several strategies for reaching out to the least educated adult were utilized: locally-oriented print materials, radio spots, television community messages, and door-to-door canvassing. The initial emphasis was on the development and testing of the "direct media production method" of producing television spots, which would portray adult basic education participants as they spontaneously discussed their experiences in the basic education program, their life situations, their accomplishments, and their expectations for the future. Because they would promote identification by viewers from the target population with the persons delivering the message, it was felt that such messages would maximize the effectiveness of mass media as a recruitment tool among this population. While those who designed this project were correct in identifying the target population as heavy television viewers, they failed to make the necessary distinction between the use of television for entertainment and its use for informational purposes.

At the conclusion of REACH, it was recognized that the results obtained were produced through the coordinated use of the several approaches, and that, as implemented by this project, the direct media approach was not cost-effective. However, the initial assumption that promoting viewer identification with the person delivering the message would enhance the effectiveness of mass media as a recruitment tool was confirmed. An evaluation of the REACH approach indicated that 30 percent of 119 ABE enrollees queried first learned of the ABE program through television, which was a close second to the 35 percent who had first heard of the program from door-to-door canvassers (McClelland, 1972). These television spots were a secondary source of information concerning the program for an additional 47 percent of the program enrollees surveyed. Only door-to-door canvassing (cited by 68 percent of respondents) was a more important secondary source of information. These figures compare favorably with the usual productivity of mass-media approaches to recruitment of the least educated. It is interesting to note that radio messages and newspaper advertisements were practically useless as a major source of information (6 percent and none, respectively), although somewhat useful as secondary sources of information (30 and 14 percent). Those reponsible for REACH concluded that television spots using these techniques would be cost-effective as a recruitment strategy when used in combination with other approaches.

Adult Armchair Education Project. The Opportunities Industrialization Center in Philadelphia employed an innovative programming approach to reach uneducated adults in an economically depressed, racially segregated area of Philadelphia (*Adult Armchair Education. . . ,* 1968). First, persons were recruited into "armchair" courses which met for ten weeks in a neighborhood home (these served as "feeder" or "vestibule" classes to ease transition to a more formal setting). These courses introduced adults to a learning experience without requiring them to leave their neighborhoods and enter an unfamiliar and possibly hostile environment. Second, these classes were open to anyone in the immediate neighborhood who wished to attend, not only to those with severe educational handicaps. Third, the learning group addressed itself to learning related to consumer problems and community action for problem solving, as well as to basic skills. The door-to-door canvassing provided a personal touch, as did word-of-mouth grapevines, often centering around the individual who agreed to act as hostess (or, in rare instances, host) for a learning group.

In contrast to almost every other project of this type, the Adult Armchair Project significantly exceeded its recruitment goal. During the period the project operated, it reached out to 892 individuals who joined in eighty courses or study groups, compared to their goal of reaching 450 in forty-five groups. On the other hand, this project was not notably successful in reaching out to males in the target population, possibly because both recruiters and hostesses tended to be female. Referrals from outside groups provided only a small percentage of the total number reached, and these were not representative of the hard-core group, which this project was most successful in reaching.

Program Organizing Related Family Instruction in the Neighborhood. POR-FIN used paraprofessional recruiters, who in some instances also taught courses. All recruiters were bilingual, because they were recruiting in a Spanish-speaking neighborhood. Individuals in the target neighborhoods were recruited to attend regular basic education or English as a Second Language courses in the community center serving their neighborhood. During one phase of this project, an experiment was conducted to assess the effectiveness of this personalized recruiting approach. One hundred sixty-five adults, parents of children enrolled in a single school, were the study population. Half of the households received only flyers, or heard of the program through word-of-mouth. Half were contacted utilizing the interview procedure devised by the POR-FIN project. This procedure consisted of an initial interview, a follow-up interview, and a second follow-up interview two weeks later. Only two of the eighty-five parents in the control group enrolled in the program, while thirty of the eighty parents in the group that was actively recruited by home visitors enrolled. In addition, twenty others in that group indicated that they intended to enroll, and another portion were not eligible to enroll because of their relatively high level of educational attainment. While there was a significant dropout rate from among those recruited, this rate varied substantially, depending upon the quality of the instruction in the class attended.

The recruiters hired by POR-FIN were selected above all for their ability as listeners, people with whom the parents they contacted could talk. The major emphasis initially was on building rapport between the recruiter and the respondent. In orientation sessions recruiters learned to emphasize the persuasive and motivational aspects of their work. They were equipped with a four-part package to familiarize the respondent with the program, which was used during follow-up visits. First, there were picture folders illustrating the program, showing congenial people and places to counteract any negative or intimidating images potential participants might have of the program location and people. Second, the recruiter had available some books used in the courses, which were selected to match the learning level of the respondent. These were intended to familiarize the respondent with the program and to ease unrealistic fears. The location and schedule of courses were dramatized through use of a sound-on-slide instructional aid called a Language Master. This served a secondary purpose of introducing the respondent to a piece of equipment used in the instructional program. Finally, the recruiter did not approach a particular individual or household "cold," but rather drew on whatever knowledge was available about the community, neighborhood, or family being approached. Particularly during the initial interview, the emphasis was on listening and garnering information concerning the respondent's needs, problems, and goals. This information served as a base for later conversations and was used to tailor arguments to be used with that person concerning the potential advantages of returning to school. In addition, recruiters were equipped with concrete information and were able to give assistance to their contacts, such as in getting needed social services. This ability to offer pragmatic information was an important ingredient in their success.

Three Strategies

Mass Media. The mass media, television, radio, and newspapers, are sometimes used as part of an overall campaign to reach out to the least educated adults (Walden, 1975). While a media awareness campaign may make a contribution to the overall outreach effort, there are distinct limits to what may be expected from these techniques, as well as some important tasks they can accomplish.

A study conducted in Ohio in the late sixties (Snyder, 1971) indicated that media messages did create awareness of the adult basic education program. Overall, 88 percent of those surveyed recalled seeing information concerning the program in the newspapers, 57 percent recalled radio announcements, and 15 percent recalled television spots. However, only 18 percent of basic education students had learned of the ABE program through these media. These statisics suggested that public awareness messages should be aimed at all segments of the population, not just at potential participants. Community residents generally should be informed concerning the benefits that basic education learners may derive from participation. Their assistance in identifying, recruiting, and referring students to the basic education program should be solicited. Such broadly aimed public awareness messages may produce results in the form of support from political, social, and religious leaders.

Mass-media announcements may serve to reassure members of the target population that they are not alone in lacking basic skills or necessary credentials. Mass-media campaigns may also be designed to provide more specific information concerning program enrollment opportunities. A project in Iowa in 1971 utilized two different ways of conveying this information, one distinctly more effective than the other (Des Moines Public Schools, 1971). During an initial phase of the BEAM (Basic Education Action Motivation) Project, spot announcements were prepared and broadcast over radio and television using free public service time. A single text was prepared for statewide use. Listeners and viewers were given a toll-free number they could call to get specific information concerning the schedule of classes in their own geographic area. This recruitment effort, over several months, produced fewer than eighty calls from the whole state. In revising their approach, project staff prepared multiple announcements, each giving specific information concerning the location, cost, sponsor, type of class offered, and phone number for that program. Fewer announcements were broadcast in any given area, but each was localized. This approach proved more effective. However, the overall conclusion of those involved with this project was that the use of radio and television as recruitment devices for basic education programs was ineffective.

A different approach was taken by the REACH project described earlier. Television spots were produced with real basic education learners telling their unrehearsed, true life stories. More recently, a similar highly localized recruitment package was developed for use in the Springfield, Massachusetts, area (Rossman, 1971). The results indicated that this approach to conveying information concerning basic education programs produces some results. An evaluation of the effort indicated that almost 20 pecent of basic education participants who enrolled during the time these experimental media messages were shown attributed their decision to enroll directly to the media package, more than twice the percentage produced by prior mass-media announcements.

Newspaper advertisements are less effective and more expensive than well-written news stories concerning the program and its students. Feature stories serve the dual purpose of reaching potential participants, as well as others in the community who may be able to identify potential participants and encourage them to participate in the program. An effective news story begins with a lead that answers the basic questions: who, what, when, where, why, and how. The lead is followed by the body of the story, which expands upon the lead. The story should be accurate, written in common language, short enough to hold the reader's attention but long enough to describe the program accurately. Including names and pictures of participants and others involved with the program is helpful.

Flyers are another mass-distributed recruitment device. They may reach households that do not get newspapers. A particularly effective means of distributing flyers is having children take them home from school, although they may be handed out in any location where people gather. Flyers should be short, simple, and attractive. They should be in color, so they will stand out from other papers, and a size that is convenient, yet will not get lost too easily. Program personnel may wish to distribute flyers personally, or may have them distributed by others.

Although the projects mentioned above have had some success in utilizing mass media in recruiting the least educated, program administrators should be aware that by and large these approaches are not particularly effective in reaching the target group. A 1969 survey in the southwest (HEW Region VI) indicated that only 2.3 percent of those adults with less than an eighth-grade education participated in basic education that year. An intensive one-month recruitment effort in Bexar County, Texas, which included the distribution of 10,000 bilingual circulars through the schools, radio and television announcements and programs, announcements at church services, housing projects, and basic education classes produced only seventy-five enrollees out of a potential population of 80,000 (Bexar County Adult Continuing Education, 1972).

Why mass-media approaches are relatively ineffective in reaching this group can be understood in terms of the adoption process model of changed social behavior. This model presents a five-stage sequence of the change process: awareness, interest, evaluation, trial, and adoption. While this model suggests that mass media may be somewhat effective in producing awareness, it also indicates that the mass-media approach is not usually sufficient in the later stages in the change process. Although a situation-specific presentation utilizing current participants will encourage identification between potential participants and those conveying the message, it does not allow for a two-way communication of ideas, questions, and concerns. This is important during the evaluation phase, which is of necessity highly personal, and is often one in which peers are very influential. Indeed, as one experienced basic education administrator has summarized the situation, "Every successful program of recruitment in the United States has relied primarily upon a personal invitation to attend the classes from a member of the student's own peer group" (Mulvey, 1969, p. 2).

Referrals. Interagency referrals are another potential source of participants in educational programs serving the least educated. Referrals have a double value in that the educational program reaches out to potential participants who might not otherwise enroll and also refers back to the agencies those participants who are in need of services provided by that agency. A statewide study of recruitment in Iowa found that agency referral was the single most effective recruitment tool among those used in urban areas (Iowa State Department of Instruction, 1974). An important condition of effective referrals is that partner agencies be kept up-to-date concerning course schedules and locations to prevent referring agencies and individuals from losing their credibility and effectiveness. A study of three basic education programs in the Northeast (Albany, New York; Bergen County, New Jersey; and White Plains, New York) that rely heavily on referral as a recruitment technique indicated that these programs generated 55 to 70 percent of their enrollments from referrals. The number of agencies with which they had linkages ranged from thirty-one to seventy-three, and the number of referrals ranged from an average of seventy to 350 per month (Beder and Smith, 1977).

Administrators who are seeking to develop a productive referral relationship with community agencies should do their homework prior to approaching the agency. What are the aims and goals of the community agency? How are they related to those of the basic education program? Answers to these questions will enable the continuing educator to identify ways in which the agencies might be of service to the educational program and, more importantly, ways that the educational program might be seen as assisting the agency which it is approaching. Once the potential benefits on both sides are listed, the administrator is ready to speak with someone at the agency. It is important to contact the right person, who is able to make the necessary decisions to implement a referral relationship. Educators must be sensitive to the needs, concerns, and priorities of the potential referring agency and recognize that they will often differ from their own. These differences should be taken into account in developing a working relationship with the agency. Educators should be patient in seeking cooperation and assistance, but also assertive in making their own requests.

The number of potential sources of referrals is almost limitless. One urban continuing educator compiled the following list: immigration and naturalization, ministerial alliance, public schools, union leaders, United Fund, barbers and hairdressers, service clubs, milkmen and breadmen, private schools, newsboys, veterans' organizations, insurance agents, speakers' bureau, local politicians, public busing authority, storekeepers, vocational rehabilitation, attendance officers, racial and nationality organizations, school census takers, welfare agencies, drivers examiners, public health agencies, physicians, law enforcement agencies, police officers, state employment service, Social Security Administration, community action committee, family court, area vocational centers, chamber of commerce, public library, and mental health centers.

An important caveat is that government agencies may not have the trust of potential program participants, and should be used with care. Employers and labor unions, on the other hand, offer the advantage of a built-in cheering section in the form of the new learner's fellow workers and employer.

A national study of adult basic education (Mezirow, Darkenwald, and Knox, 1975) found that the least educated and most in need of educational services generally do not use the mass media as a source of information for solving problems and that, while they may be in contact with community agencies, few will take advice from other than their closest friends. Their contacts with agencies are neither sustained nor formalized, so that few can be reached through cosponsorship arrangements. This suggests that referrals alone may not reach members of the real hard-core population.

Recruiters. The Appalachian Adult Education Project found that 90 percent of the adult basic education participants they served had learned of and been motivated to attend basic education courses from personal sources: recruiters (46 percent), friends (14 percent), family (5 percent), and "other personal" (25 percent) (Snyder, 1971, p. 11). In recording the effectiveness of various types of recruiters, they found that trained basic education teacher-recruiters brought 57 percent of their contacts into the program. Lay recruiters brought in 28 percent of contacts, and public school teachers, only 18 percent.

Capable recruiters are essential to the ultimate productivity of the recruitment effort. The best recruiters share certain characteristics and have received orientation in the procedures necessary for effective recruiting. In general, they may be characterized as stable, enthusiastic, and aggressive. They need to be able to withstand rebuff and to cope with despondency and anger, both their own and others'. They need to be interested in people and accepting of others, as well as patient and dependable. They need to be committed and concerned about people, willing to exert an effort to help someone. It is desirable that they represent the racial and cultural elements of the community, and best if they are in fact from that community. Finally, they must be articulate and able to communicate effectively to those with whom they come in contact as a result of their work.

Successful recruiters may include basic education students and former students, as well as local paraprofessionals. Ministers, teachers, social workers, and others who work with the least educated and believe in the value of education may also be effective. Regardless of background, the effective recruiter must be an excellent salesperson, who will not take no for an answer. In general, those most responsible for implementation of the actual instructional program are most effective. Experience in the Appalachian region of Georgia suggests that 80 per-

cent or more of those recruited by basic education teachers or paraprofessionals remain in the program (Orr and Yeatts, 1970).

A national study of urban basic education programs found that
over 40 percent of large urban programs used local community personnel on a part-time basis as recruiters (Mezirow, Darkenwald, and
Knox, 1975). These individuals were usually already working in the
community or neighborhood. Their roles might be as social workers,
teachers, or religious leaders. Once they were oriented to the basic education program, they worked in the area in their own way. The identification and recruitment services they performed for the basic education program complemented rather than displaced their other work.
They were particularly effective in recruiting for the basic education
program because they could draw on an existing network of contacts,
and were in the community many hours of the day and week. Such indig-
enous workers may operate highly independently of the program and
get heavily involved with the problems and situations of those with
whom they are working. They are then effectively out of the control of
the program administrator. However, most directors felt that the possible advantages of operating on this basis were outweighed by the
incomparable recruiting effectiveness resulting from their work.

Prior to actively recruiting individuals into the program, an
outreach person must identify those in the community who are in need
of the educational services provided by the basic education program. In
providing orientation for outreach personnel, it is important to include
this component. Potential participants may be identified in a variety of
ways. Social service agencies may be able and willing to share the
names and addresses of those utilizing their services. Such agencies
include welfare, employment, housing, and children's services. Additional sources of names include a door-to-door survey, and current and
former basic education participants.

In addition to using newspapers, radio, and television to reach
those who might refer others to the program, posters, pamphlets, and
flyers can be designed for this purpose. The educator may also make personal presentations before community groups such as the parent association, service organizations, and business groups.

Potential participants should be contacted personally as soon as
possible after they have been identified as needing the educational services provided by the program, or when they have expressed an interest
in learning more about the program. The initial personal interview is
critical to continued contact with the potential participant and to fostering a decision to actually enroll in the program. Recruiters should
establish rapport with the persons with whom they are talking. This
means responding appropriately to the cultural orientation and socioeconomic status and concerns of potential participants. Once rapport is

established, the recruiter must often intentionally work to raise the low self-concept of the individual. If the potential participants do not honestly believe they have the capacity to achieve, then arguments concerning the potential value of educational achievement will not influence the potential enrollee. Belief in their ability to achieve, as well as a desire to achieve, are critical if adults are to make the decision to enroll. The recruiter may need to work to instill each of these attitudes. As this process proceeds, the recruiter will want to provide for the identification of worthwhile and attainable individual objectives by the undereducated adult, and relate attainment of these objectives to participation in the continuing education program.

Once the potential participants view the continuing education program as relevant to their situations, abilities, and goals, then the recruiter can concentrate on delivering important information about the program itself. First, the recruiter should make clear the purpose of the program: to assist persons in educational, vocational, and social advancement within their community. The program may enable participants to be more effective as parents, consumers, citizens, employees. It may assist participants in more successfully solving daily problems, or in attaining the high school equivalency certificate. In this part of the message, the recruiter is reinforcing the relationship between participating in the educational program and the potential participant's own concerns, aspirations, and goals. A second piece of information that the recruiter should include is eligibility requirements for entering the program. In particular, questions of age and access for handicapped participants should be honestly stated. Should unexpected barriers to participation arise because this information was not correctly conveyed, the recruiter's subsequent ability to operate in that community will be damaged.

Third, the recruiter should identify all of the potentially suitable educational programs at each location in the local area. Specific and correct information should be given concerning the alternative locations and schedules available. Another type of information that may support the potential participant's decision to enroll is information about what to expect. This would include, for example, the extent to which the program utilizes a diagnostic-prescriptive approach to individualization, the availability of counseling and education regarding life skills, and the relative emphasis on individual, small-group, and whole-class instruction and learning. Potential participants should have some idea how much flexibility is allowed in scheduling class work or selecting what type of learning activity to pursue. They should be informed of all available options, including home instruction and individual tutoring.

Programming

A national study of basic education concluded that if the least educated adult population was to be reached, it would be necessary to set aside a portion of available funds specifically for this purpose (Mezirow, Darkenwald, and Knox, 1975). These funds would support a specially planned strategy for recruitment, staff selection and orientation, instruction, and support services, probably with a higher unit cost per continuing participant. A more recent position paper prepared for the Ford Foundation (Hunter and Harman, 1979) argues that the most extremely handicapped will be reached only through community-based strategies emphasizing the identification and solution of community problems by persons within their communities. Both reports point to the need to consider significant changes in programming in order to reach and retain the least educated. Each demonstrates the inadequacy of concentrating on improved recruitment techniques alone if these least educated adults are to enroll in continuing education programs.

Two approaches have been used to cushion the transition into the continuing education setting: individual tutoring and small feeder or vestibule courses. Use of these approaches in familiar and comfortable settings such as the home or workplace tends to encourage continued attendance. In 1979, Ohio and Florida, among others, sponsored special state projects utilizing these strategies. Past experience with the vestibule approach was described earlier, in the discussion of the Philadelphia Adult Armchair Project. Programs utilizing home tutoring have included the Appalachian Adult Education Demonstration Project and the Homebound Project in Butte, Montana (Butte Vocational Technical Center, 1973; Way and Moore, 1975).

Utilizing such strategies as a temporary measure is desirable. Community outreach courses, though they have the advantage of familiar setting and ethnic or racial homogeneity, may also suffer from extreme variation in achievement levels, which makes their educational effectiveness problematical. Temporary feeder courses reap the benefits and avoid the worst of the disadvantages. If they are available, it is important to assign aides and volunteers to such courses in order to deal with continuous enrollment and varying achievement levels among participants. The teacher should also be aware of instructional strategies that will capitalize on this variation. In addition, because the purpose of this transition phase is to provide orientation to the more formal ecucation program, and to develop strategies for coping with barriers to participation, such as childcare problems, transportation needs, health concerns, and employment conflicts, teachers should have special skills and sensitivities.

Programming innovations designed to emphasize problem identification and problem-solving action require new approaches to needs assessment, staff orientation, the design of curricular materials, and the organization and evaluation of instruction. One project that has attempted to move in this direction developed instructional materials utilizing visuals from students' communities. Visuals and accompanying narrative materials were selected and developed on the basis of interviews, in which adults identified community characteristics and problems and expressed directly and indirectly their beliefs, values, and attitudes concerning their community. The instructional process incorporated open-ended discussion, in which learners could begin to identify particular goals, problems, and strategies for action. This approach did result in participant learning and action distinctive from that normally found in basic education courses, and in changes in participants' self-perceptions and social interaction patterns (Irish, 1975). Available data do not allow definitive statements concerning the efficacy of this approach in attracting and retaining the least educated; however, anecdotal evidence supports its effectiveness. Research (Darkenwald, 1975) does suport the concept that instruction focusing on proficiency in areas such as consumer education, health, community resources, and employment tends to promote retention, particularly if such instruction is provided by persons from the same sociocultural group as the learners.

References

Adult Armchair Education Program: Final Report, June 1967–March 1968. Philadelphia, Penn.: Opportunities Industrialization Center (OIC), 1968. (ERIC Document Reproduction Service ED 042 944.)

Adult Education: Section II: Survey of State Support. Washington, D.C.: National Advisory Council on Adult Education (NACAE), 1977.

Anderson, D., and Niemi, J. A. *Adult Education and the Disadvantaged Adult.* Syracuse, N.Y.: ERIC Clearinghouse on Adult Education, November 1970.

Anderson, R. E., and Darkenwald, G. G. *Participation and Persistence in American Adult Education.* New York: The College Board, 1979.

Beder, H. W., and Smith, F. B. *Developing an Adult Education Program through Community Linkages.* Washington, D.C.: Adult Education Association of the U.S.A., 1977.

Bexar County Adult Continuing Education. *POR-FIN (Program Organizing Related Family Instruction in the Neighborhood).* San Antonio, Tex., 1972.

Butte Vocational Technical Center. *309b Adult Education Act Replication Guide (Project Homebound, The Experiment at Butte and Project Prepare).* Butte, Mont., 1973. (ERIC document Reproduction Service ED 109 493.)

Catalog of Adult Education Projects Fiscal Year 1978. Washington, D.C.: Clearinghouse for Adult Education and Life Long Learning (ADELL), U.S. Government Printing Office, 1978.

Catalog of Adult Education Projects Fiscal Year 1979. Washington, D.C.: Clearinghouse for Adult Education and Life Long Learning (ADELL), U.S. Government Printing Office, 1979.

Darkenwald, G. G. "Some Effects of the 'Obvious Variable': Teachers' Race and Holding Power with Black Adult Students." *Sociology of Education,* 1975, *48,* 420–431.

Des Moines Public Schools. *Project BEAM (Basic Education Action Motivation) Final Evaluation Report.* Des Moines, Iowa, 1971. (ERIC Document Reproduction Service ED 101 106.)

Hunter, C. S., and Harman, D. *Adult Illiteracy in the United States.* New York: McGraw-Hill, 1979.

Iowa State Department of Instruction. *A Handbook for Recruiting: Adult Basic Education: Iowa.* Des Moines, Iowa, 1974. (ERIC Document Reproduction Service ED 105 285.)

Irish, G. H. "Reflections on Ends and Means in Adult Basic Education." *Adult Education,* 1975, *25* (2), 125–130.

McClelland, S. D. *Project REACH: Final Report, Year Two.* South Bend, Ind.: University of Notre Dame, 1972. (ERIC Document Reproduction Service ED 101 104.)

Mezirow, J. D., Darkenwald, G. G., and Knox, A. B. *Last Gamble on Education.* Washington, D.C.: Adult Education Association of the U.S.A., 1975.

Mezirow, J. D., and Irish, G. H. *Priorities for Experimentation and Demonstration.* Vol. 1: *Innovations for Change in Adult Basic Education.* New York: Center for Adult Education, Columbia University, 1974.

Mulvey, M. C. *Recruitment in Adult Basic Education, Handbook.* Prepared for the New England Regional Adult Education Conference, Lexington, Mass.: April, 1969. (ERIC Document Reproduction Service ED 030 800.)

Orr, T. P., and Yeatts, P. *Georgia State Module Final Report.* Morehead, Ky.: Appalachian Adult Education Center, Morehead State University, June, 1970. (ERIC Document Reproduction Service ED 054 417.)

Rossman, M. H. *A Model to Recruit Functionally Illiterate Adults into Adult Basic Education Programs in Massachusetts.* Amherst: School of Education, University of Massachusetts, 1971. (ERIC Document Reproduction Service ED 064 589.)

Snyder, R. E. *Recruitment in Adult Basic Education.* Tallahassee: Research Information Processing Center, 1971. (ERIC Document Reproduction Service ED 079 584.)

Walden, B. L. *Recruitment and Retention of the Adult Learner.* Montgomery: Alabama State Department of Education, June 1975. (ERIC Document Reproduction Service ED 112 075.)

Way, M., and Moore, S. *Helping Adults Learn: A Handbook for Home Instruction Paraprofessionals in Adult Basic Education.* Morehead, Ky.: Appalachian Adult Education Center, Morehead State University, 1975. (ERIC Document Reproduction Service ED 112 153.)

Gladys H. Irish is director for program planning, analysis, and evaluation, Office of Continuing Education, Kingsborough Community College, City University of New York. From 1971 to 1973, she was an associate at the Center for Adult Education, Teachers College, Columbia University. She served as an associate director with the Apperception Interaction Method (AIM): Practical Action Literacy Project from 1973 to 1975.

Even some highly educated professionals can be hard-to-reach
learners. New and better approaches to needs assessment
and the delivery of educational services are essential
if real progress is to be made.

Encouraging Continuing
Education for Professionals

Craig L. Scanlan

Continuing Professional Education (CPE) includes any purposeful,
systematic, and sustained effort conducted by professionals after completion of their entry-level education to update or expand the proficiency, knowledge, skills, or attitudes necessary to effectively discharge
their occupational roles.

CPE is the fastest-growing segment of continuing education. Of
the many reasons for this growth, the postindustrial trend toward pro-
fessionalization of the work force is the most important. The near-
exponential increase in the growth rate of new knowledge has created
societal demands for specialized expertise. The result of such demands
has been the growth and proliferation of service and technologically oriented professional occupations in which the application of a complex body
of knowledge is both the medium of exchange and the *raison d'être*. Since
1950, the professional work force in the United States has more than
doubled, now representing more than 10 percent of the total employed
population.

It is ironic that the very factors responsible for the rise of the
expert represent the most potent threats to the continuity of professional proficiency. As the professional work force grows, so too does the
recognition that specialized knowledge is a perishable commodity, that
the skills and attitudes acquired during preparatory education are sub-

ject to rapid obsolescence, and that only by maintaining a lifelong commitment to learning can professionals expect to remain proficient and fulfill their increasingly complex obligations to their occupations, their clients and employers, and the society they serve.

Participation in CPE

Clearly, society has a stake in the continuing ability of professionals to effectively discharge their occupations and responsibilities. Both governmental support and regulation of CPE have increased dramatically in the last decade. In addition, public scrutiny of professional proficiency is increasing. Litigation and legislation are focusing on ensuring that professional services are competently delivered.

Nowhere are these trends more evident that in the growth in participation in formal CPE. Between 1969 and 1975, the number of part-time participants in CPE courses increased by 72 percent and the number of actual offerings geared to the needs of the professional work force nearly doubled (National Center for Education Statistics, 1978). It is not surprising that the participation rate for professionals in continuing education (34 percent) is the highest of adult learners—nearly three times that of the adult population in general and more than twice that of all occupational groups combined.

Despite the comparative success of CPE in attracting a large proportion of its target population, viewed from the perspective of a society increasingly dependent upon the delivery of professional services by providers subject to functional obsolescence, the picture is less encouraging (Knox, 1979a). Despite the remarkable growth in the availability of CPE programming, fully two-thirds of the nation's professional work force remains untouched by formal CPE activities each year. Although nonparticipation in formal CPE cannot be construed to categorically indicate lack of motivation or involvement in learning, the large size of this hard-to-reach professional population should be of concern both to members of the educational community and to society. If CPE is to have any impact upon the proficiency of the professional work force and the quality of the services it renders, efforts must be made to identify the characteristics of hard-to-reach professionals and develop strategies to encourage their participation in lifelong learning.

Health Professions Continuing Education

For program planners intent on reaching the hard-to-reach professional, the health professions represent a particularly appropriate model for scrutiny. The general goals, educational resources, and program development processes of continuing education in the health fields are similar to those of CPE in general. In addition, factors influencing the delivery of health professions continuing education (such as the diversified nature of services; the emergence of semiprofessional occupational groups; the impact of technology; and the growing influence of educational institutions, professional associations, and the federal and state governments) are common to other professional fields. Of particular importance to the CPE planner is the growing body of descriptive and motivational research on participants in health professions continuing education. No other professional category has as long a tradition of CPE nor has undergone as close a scrutiny as medicine and its related disciplines, and in no other field have so many diverse efforts been made to reach those reluctant or unable to participate.

Goals of CPE in Health Care. The ultimate goal of health professions continuing education is to improve the quality of health care. The fundamental assumption guiding planners of CPE for health professionals is that practitioner participation in systematic and sustained learning efforts will improve care. A simple corollary to this assumption is that health professionals who do not participate in continuing education risk obsolescence and therefore represent a potential threat to the quality of the delivery system. Despite the apparent logic of such assumptions, a direct link between CPE and the quality of health care delivery has yet to be consistently demonstrated (Lloyd and Abrahamson, 1979). There is evidence that well-designed continuing education activities can have an impact on improved performance (Knox, 1979b). It has been more difficult to demonstrate an effect of professional performance on society, such as in improved patient health. The failure to empirically demonstrate any significant improvement in care may represent the most important deterrent to practitioner involvement. Clearly, a comprehensive strategy to encourage professional participation must be based on efforts to demonstrate its efficacy. Until such evidence is provided, professionals, who demand results from planned intervention, will remain skeptical.

Target Population. Over four million people were actively employed in the health care industry in 1970; manpower is expected to more than double by 1990 (U.S. Department of Health, Education, and Welfare, 1974). Represented among the health manpower pool are the four traditional professional categories (physicians, dentists, pharmacists, and nurses) and a growing number of aspiring professional groups categorized under the rubric "allied health occupations." Not represented in the statistical data are the substantial numbers of health personnel currently inactive but planning to return to practice during their lifetime. Consisting primarily of women who have temporarily left the work force to assume the responsibilities of parenthood, this group of inactive professionals represents an additional and important segment of a continuing education market which is large, diverse, and growing.

The Hard-to-Reach Health Professional

Continuing education agencies, health professional occupational groups, and society in general have differing perspectives on who is the hard-to-reach professional. For the agency offering continuing education, the hard-to-reach professional is the nonparticipant in its programming; for the professional group representing the practitioner, it is the laggard who fails to adopt and incorporate relevant new knowledge and skills into the delivery of services; for society in general, it is the provider whose substandard proficiency or outright obsolescence potentially endangers the public safety or welfare. Each perspective has its merits and they are interrelated. More often than not, however, participation patterns form the basis for defining the hard-to-reach professional. Only recently have assessments of motivational orientations and attitudes and assessment of proficiency been employed to identify the hard to reach.

Magnitude of the Problem. Nakamoto and Verner (1973), after reviewing a decade of literature on continuing education in the health professions, pessimistically concluded that the members of the disciplines studied were not deeply committed to learning to maintain their professional proficiency. Despite the increased availability of CPE and the flurry of licensing regulations and associations and specialty board mandates for continuing education that characterized the seventies, fully one-third or more of health professionals recently studied reported no formal continuing education participation (Arndt, DeMuth, and Weinswig, 1975; Broski and Upp, 1979; Kubat, 1975; Lewis and Hassanein, 1970).

Profile of the Hard-to-Reach Professional. Most of what we know about the hard-to-reach has been inferred from studies of participants. Four general approaches, used singly or in combination, are commonly employed: descriptive research, assessment of motivational orientations, measurement of proficiency or obsolescence, and determination of barriers to participation.

Although generalizations regarding the descriptive characteristics of hard-to-reach professionals are somewhat discipline-specific, the picture that emerges is relatively consistent (Nakamoto and Verner, 1973). Nonparticipants tend to be older and less educated or less qualified than participants. Many nonparticipants are geographically isolated or lack access to instructional resources and most exhibit minimal involvement in professional activities other than the responsibilities of the job itself. Among those employed by health care agencies, health professionals not participating in continuing education tend to hold part-time or nonsupervisory staff positions providing general (as opposed to specialized) services. The lowest rate of participation in continuing education occurs among health professionals who are inactive but plan to return to practice or those otherwise removed from direct involvement in health care delivery.

Motivational orientations and attitudes are being identified as among the most significant factors determining the nature and magnitude of professionals' efforts to update and maintain their proficiency. Clark and Dickinson (1976) confirmed that motivational and attitudinal factors were better predictors of nurses' participation in continuing education than descriptive characteristics. They also demonstrated that low learning efforts were correlated with negative attitudes toward CPE and low professional, interactive, and learning orientations. Burgess (1976) revealed that the magnitude of learner participation in CPE was directly related to both self-esteem and career aspiration; nurses holding low opinions of themselves, who did not aspire to more responsible positions within the field, tended to have low rates of participation. Finally, Bevis (1975) demonstrated that for employed professional nurses the conflict inherent in trying to simultaneously adhere to both a bureaucratic and a service role exerts a distinct negative influence on CPE participation.

Assessment of proficiency is among the newest of the methods employed to identify the hard-to-reach professional. By providing evidence of the magnitude of individual or group functional obsolescence, assessment of proficiency can differentiate between the true laggard population and those nonparticipants who successfully employ alternative, self-directed methods to update their professional knowledge and skills. Although fraught with methodological difficulties, proficiency assessment techniques have provided valuable insight into factors associated with obsolescence and have confirmed many prior speculative assumptions regarding the "hard-core" of recalcitrant professionals (Le Breton, 1979). Evidence from both nursing (Kubat, 1975) and pharmacy (Gross, 1975) indicates that the least proficient professionals tend to be older, part-time practitioners living in small or geographically isolated communities. They characteristically hold comparatively low levels of formal education, are less professionally oriented than others, and exhibit low participation rates in continuing education.

Studies of barriers to participation yield useful insight into the characteristics of the hard-to-reach professional. Major deterrents to participation identified by Nakamoto and Verner (1973) in medicine, pharmacy, dentistry, and nursing have been substantiated by more recent research in the emerging health professions (Broski and Upp, 1979). Among health professionals in general, situational factors tend to be reported as the most significant category of barriers to participation. Work responsibilities (to employer or clients) and family responsibilities predominate, with family responsibilities being most significant among female professionals with preschool-age children. Factors related to sponsoring institutions' programming represent secondary but significant deterrents to participation: distance, cost, inconvenient scheduling, dubious relevance or lack of quality courses or programs are the most frequently cited obstacles. Informational barriers, less often reported, are nonetheless significant to program planners. Insufficient advance notice or inadequate publicity were commonly cited, with insufficient advance notice being a particularly potent obstacle among institutionally employed professionals who must arrange leave time in order to attend CPE offerings. Attitudinal and motivational factors are seldom addressed by surveys of obstacles to participation. Only poor past experiences with CPE (discouragement with its irrelevance, inefficiency, or ineffectiveness) and the belief that it is hard to learn after a certain age are noteworthy. Unfortunately, the relative insignificance of the attitudinal barriers is misleading. Only recently has the potential influence of motivational orientations and attitudes on participation among professionals been ambitiously investigated.

Categories of Hard-to-Reach Professionals. The present evidence suggests that hard-to-reach professionals do not constitute a homogeneous group with singular characteristics. Indeed, the genus "hard-to-reach professional" may include at least three distinct species, each with unique attributes, attributes critically important to program planners intent upon gaining their participation. Categories of hard-to-reach professionals emerging from the literature include:

- *The "Hard-Core" Laggards,* including the older, isolated, or otherwise uninvolved professionals who lack the personal initiative to continue their learning and underestimate the impact of new knowledge upon their discipline, thus risking functional incompetence and professional obsolescence.
- *The Constrained Professionals,* including those who would participate, but for whom significant situational, institutional, informational, or attitudinal barriers discourage active engagement in sponsored learning activities.
- *The Innovators or Pacesetters,* including professionals working at the forefronts of new knowledge in their disciplines, who, discouraged with the irrelevance, inefficiency, dubious effectiveness, or inflexibility of traditional CPE programming, implement and plan their own learning activities to meet their own learning needs.

Strategies designed to reach the hard-to-reach professional must recognize and respond to differences among these categories.

Strategies to Reach the Hard-to-Reach Health Professional

If attitudes, learning orientations, and role conceptions are important influences on participation in CPE, then the influence of professionals' preparatory education may be the most important determinant of their approaches to lifelong learning. Most new professionals are ill-prepared to assume responsibility for this task (Schein, 1972). Only by encouraging professional students to desire and develop the skills necessary to engage in lifelong, self-directed education can a mutually complementary linkage be established between the preparatory and continuing education of the professional (Knox, 1974).

Until this goal is achieved, planners of CPE will continue to be faced with a substantial population of hard-to-reach professionals. Meanwhile, efforts to articulate professional preparatory and continuing education must be complemented with strategies designed to encourage and facilitate the participation of would-be learners who are otherwise reluctant or unable to continue their education. Such strategies may be broadly categorized into those designed to (1) maximize the relevance of planned learning activities, (2) minimize barriers to learner participation, (3) address the special needs of the self-directed learner, and (4) improve the visibility and desirability of the program offerings.

Maximizing Relevance. The unique identifying trait of the professional is the ability to translate a complex body of knowledge into practice. Thus, the learning activities most likely to gain the support of health professionals are those which are perceived as being immediately practical and directly applicable to their particular practice situations (Nakamoto and Verner, 1973). Although assuring that educational activities are relevant to the needs of potential participants is a basic tenet of continuing education, more often than not the principle is not achieved in practice.

Learning activities are relevant to the extent that their intended outcomes fulfill an identified need related to the professional's practice. A need is simply a real or perceived disparity between the professional's current level of practice and that which is expected or desired. Needs assessment, when properly implemented, serves two complementary purposes: it provides the educational planner with a means for validly selecting the educational objectives of a learning episode, and it provides a practical basis for motivating the learner to engage in the educational process (Knox, 1974). Assessing clientele needs is not only a key element in the design and implementation of quality CPE programming; it is also a necessary strategy in attracting the hard-to-reach professional.

Educational needs may be assessed by a number of methods.

Interviews, questionnaires or surveys, tests, group problem analysis, job analysis performance review, and record audits are the techniques most often employed to assess occupational learning needs (Knowles, 1970). Within the health professions, surveys, tests, job analysis, and record audits are the most commonly utilized and best described (Knox, 1974). CPE planners intent on reaching the hard-to-reach professional should be aware of the advantages and limitations of each method and become skilled in their selection and use (Pennington, 1980).

Survey research is among the most widely applied and least expensive of the techniques employed to identify prospective learner needs. The literature is replete with local and regional survey assessments of practicing professionals' educational needs (Nakamoto and Verner, 1973). Unfortunately, the utilization of survey research as a basis for developing relevant programs for the hard-to-reach professional is, at best, a questionable strategy. Needs assessment surveys seldom differentiate between those who characteristically participate and those who do not. Furthermore, it is likely that nonparticipants represent a high proportion of nonrespondents to needs assessment questionnaires; such nonrespondent bias would tend to provide a picture of learning activities that are popular among participants, rather than those that are needed or desired by the hard-to-reach. The most questionable aspect of needs assessment techniques conducted by survey is, however, their validity. With the evidence clearly indicating that there is little correlation between a health professional's expressed learning needs and those actually encountered in practice (Hiemstra and Long, 1974; Nakamoto and Verner, 1973), respondent preference questionnaires may only obscure real deficiencies in proficiency and result in educational programming that treats the symptoms rather than the cause of the maladies it purports to remedy.

Self-assessment inventories and proficiency tests hold multiple appeal as both incentives for learning and as planning tools for self-directed or sponsored CPE. The *self-assessment inventory* is a confidential and objective evaluation of an individual practitioner's strengths and weaknesses in a particular content category or practice area. Initially introduced in medicine as a means for self-diagnosis of educational needs, the self-assessment inventory provides practitioners with normative profiles useful in selecting and planning individually relevant learning activities. However, the motivational potential of such instruments was not unforeseen.

Large-scale administration of *proficiency tests* to the target population could provide the educational planner with the data necessary to develop programming relevant to the needs of potential participants. The research of Kubat (1975) and Gross (1975) underscores the potential utility of group testing techniques in identifying the hard-to-reach professional.

Observational methods of determining continuing professional educational needs are the most direct and potentially most valid of all needs appraisal techniques. Meyer (1970) employed observation of physicians as a basis for developing a "practice profile" of most frequently encountered patient management problems. The profile, utilized in conjunction with a test of the physician's knowledge, provided the basis for individual consultation on educational needs. Unfortunately, the use of direct observational methods as a technique of needs assessment is distinctly limited by cost.

The health care audit is considered by most educational planners to be the most potent and relevant of the needs appraisal tools used in the continuing education of the health professional (Knox, 1974). The data bases for the health care audit are the problem-oriented medical records of the practitioners themselves. After manual or automated review of common trends or patterns-of-practice problems encountered by the targeted professionals, a description of practice emerges that can be compared to set criteria of performance, thereby establishing both the nature and magnitude of educational need. The relevance of the health care audit is based on its direct and immediately practical relationship to the practitioner's day-to-day clinical activities. Its impact upon the professional is all the more significant if the individual is directly involved in the process.

Minimizing Barriers to Participation. Establishing the need for and relevance of continuing education can only frustrate professionals constrained by significant situational or institutional barriers to participation. Because many of the barriers mentioned are based on availability and access, program planners intent on reaching the constrained professional should focus their efforts on developing flexible and innovative programming strategies that can accommodate the time and place needs of the busy practitioner. Successful efforts to improve access to CPE have employed, singularly or in combination, two important strategies: offering traditional formats in locations and at times convenient to the potential participants, and utilizing nontraditional delivery systems.

Providing traditional formats flexibly scheduled in time and place is a particularly effective strategy for reaching professionals who are geographically isolated and unable to afford the time or cost involved in extensive travel. The problem for such professionals is compounded by a scarcity of traditional academic resources, the limited ability of small health care facilities to provide effective CPE and the small aggregate numbers of practitioners available to support planned educational activities (Bennett, 1979).

Strategies successful in overcoming these significant problems have focused on developing local or regional linkages between university centers and community hospital and health care agencies (Manning and others, 1979). Properly designed, such "outreach" programs employ the expertise of university-based planners in the development and implementation of educational activities based upon the specific needs of the targeted professional group. Care is taken to involve the potential participants early in the planning stages of the program, and efforts are made to utilize local resources to reinforce those provided by the university. The linkage concept has the distinct advantage of providing access to resources not normally available to the institution or its professional staff, and as long as the goals of the learning activities are indeed based upon the identified needs of the participants, such programming should be both relevant and immediately applicable to the local practitioner's role and function.

The ability of such linkage programs to attract a significant proportion of the targeted population is one measure of their success. Over 60 percent of those targeted for the University of Southern California's Community Hospital Network consortium participated in at least one of its outreach offerings (Manning and others, 1979), and 80 percent of the physicians invited to attend the University of Colorado Medical Center's extramural program in emergency care participated (Owens and others, 1979). Preliminary findings on such outreach programs also indicate both a high degree of participant satisfaction, and, of utmost significance, successful achievement of learner outcomes. An additional practical benefit is the cost effectiveness of linkage arrangements. By joining in consortia with universities, community hospitals are able to provide quality educational programming to their professional staffs, which was previously fiscally impossible.

The development and utilization of innovative nontraditional educational delivery systems has provided program planners with additional ways to increase access to continuing education activities. The new communications technologies described earlier by Larson offer particular appeal in minimizing barriers to participation among professionals whose time constraints exclude all but the most flexible of educational scheduling. Communications media techniques such as two-way telelecture, dial access phone consultation networks and broadcast, and cable or microwave television have all been employed in health professions continuing education (Charters and Blakely, 1974; Denne and others, 1972).

Although the potential utility of such delivery systems in disseminating information is clear, the literature provides little evidence of its effectiveness. Program planners knowledgeable of the high cost and lack of proved efficacy of communications media in continuing education are justifiably cautious in its implementation. Clearly, many of the problems thus far encountered with the new media are related to inappropriateness of the format chosen or a lack of attention in design to the basic principles of adult education. However, rather than abandoning the utilization of communications media as a means of providing access to learning for hard-to-reach professionals, program planners should develop the skills necessary to ensure its appropriate utilization. Its present growth is already providing the technological basis for an expansive and readily accessible educational network of unparalleled dimensions. With the growing acceptance among health professionals of the capabilities of the new media, and the knowledge that typically 90 percent or more of those surveyed would willingly participate in CPE if it were offered in the home (Nakamoto and Verner, 1973), major new efforts are needed to fulfill the promise of communications technologies in reaching the hard-to-reach (Chamberlain, 1980).

Supplementing the developments in the application of communications media to continuing education are advances in educational technology. Whereas the communications media focus on widespread dissemination of knowledge, educational technology emphasizes both flexibility of usage and individuality of application. Programmed instruction, audio- and videotape packages, self-study modules and computer-assisted instruction are presently the primary formats for providing individual continuing educational opportunties to professionals. Professional associations have played a key role in the development and dissemination of such learning resources. Offering modular or packaged learning programs as supplements to the traditional fare of lectures, workshops, and symposia provides planner and learner alike with many options to meet a variety of needs. Such efforts are noteworthy in their recognition of the changing role of the continuing professional educator and provider agency. Clearly, as the number and diversity of educational options increases, linking the learner to the appropriate learning resources will become as important as planning and providing traditional instruction.

Addressing the Needs of the Self-Directed Learner. The reorientation of the traditional educator's role to that of a "linking agent" is a particulary important strategy for planners intent upon facilitating the learning activities of professionals engaged in self-directed education. That health professionals devote a significant majority of their learning efforts to self-directed pursuits is clearly established (Castle and Storey, 1968; Clark and Dickinson, 1976; Morgan, 1977). What is not often appreciated is that many of those categorized as hard to reach are indeed actively and continuously engaged in learning activities unrelated to those commonly offered by continuing education agencies. Program planners who are aware of the magnitude of such self-directed activities would be negligent not to address the special needs of this substantial population of professionals.

Simply encouraging the participation of the self-directed learner in traditional educational formats may be inappropriate and counterproductive. Knox (1974) argues that the needs of self-directed and self-motivated learners can best be met by resource personnel capable of facilitating the efforts of professionals to relate the actual problems characterizing their practice to the vast (and often individually unmanageable) knowledge resources available to them. There is substantial evidence that health professionals already utilize such linking agents or knowledge brokers. Formally establishing access to individuals trained in the linkage role would surely increase both the efficiency and relevance of professionals' self-directed learning efforts and potentially encourage the hard-to-reach to become more involved in individually tailored educational activities. For the continuing educator, such a reorientation role will require specialized preparation in educational resource management, as well as the development of sufficient content expertise to knowledgeably interact with the learners themselves.

Improving the Desirability and Visibility of Program Offerings. CPE planners attempting to attract the hard-to-reach professional should pay particular attention to the marketing strategies described earlier by Beder. Unfortunately, the remarkable growth in demand for CPE has lulled many continuing education agencies into the euphoric assumption that their product sells itself. Such a minimal marketing approach may have been appropriate a decade ago, but concurrent with the growth in demand for CPE has been an equally dramatic increase in the number of agencies offering continuing education activities for practicing professionals. For the program planner intent upon reaching the hard-to-reach professional, the problems of competition are compounded by the uncertain demand for CPE that characterizes this special target market. The knowledge that nonparticipants represent a significant and largely untapped proportion of the potential market for CPE should encourage planners to develop marketing strategies geared to the hard-to-reach professional. Agencies successful in attracting this segment of the market are likely to realize more substantial gains in participation than those who continue to compete only for traditional participants.

Desirability of program offerings can be increased by relating educational programming to the desires of the target market. *Clientele analysis* is an effective and practical means for program planners to assess the desirability of their "product line" for the market segment they wish to attract. Usually employed in conjunction with a needs assessment survey, a clientele analysis for CPE collects respondent data on preferred program attributes or characteristics (duration and scheduling of program, format, location, cost). If a representative sample is selected from the targeted market segment, rational programming decisions based upon such data should increase the desirability of program offerings for that group. Prior to implementing such procedures, however, planners should be aware that recent research indicates that clientele analysis focusing solely on the characteristics of the tangible product (as described by Beder) may be an insufficient basis for programming decisions.

Smorynski and Parochka (1979) provide evidence that the manner in which a professional decides whether to participate in a particular continuing education activity is a complex hierarchical process that goes beyond assessment of the quality and features of the tangible offering to an evaluation of the essential utility of the activity and a cost-benefit analysis of program worth. Such preliminary findings are consistent with what is known about consumers in the commercial marketplace. Program planners attempting to reach the hard-to-reach professional must take heed of such evidence and become more sophisticated in their ability to assess the orientations of their targeted clientele.

Strategies designed to increase the visibility of program offerings are becoming increasingly important as the competition for participants steadily grows. Failure of the commonly employed promotional techniques (mailed brochure, paid advertising) to attract large numbers of the hard-to-reach is due in part to emphasis only on the tangible product. New and innovative means of promoting the augmented benefits of continuing education participation are urgently needed if the reluctant are to be reached.

Unfortunately, even the best-designed promotional efforts may fail if the marketplace is oversaturated with similar advertising. The use of supplemental methods of increasing program visibility among the hard-to-reach is thus necessary and desirable. Publicity should reinforce paid advertising and be integrated with networks of planned personal contacts and incentives for participation. Personal contact is a particularly appropriate means of increasing program visibility among typically collegial groups of professionals. Where program sponsorship is shared by linkage arrangements among universities, professional associations, and health care agencies, such informal peer networks of communication are among the most effective means of promoting programs and encouraging reluctant professionals to participate. Finally, for potential participants who are goal-oriented, the offering of extrinsic incentives such as certificates, credits, recognition points, and Continuing Education Units (CEU's) increases both the visibility and desirability of programming and can serve as a powerful inducement for participation.

Trends in CPE

Many complex factors are beginning to have a significant impact upon the ability of CPE planners to reach the hard-to-reach professional. Foremost among these trends are the increasing implementation of cooperative linkage arrangements, the growth of regulatory and accrediting mechanisms, and burgeoning demands for mandatory participation in CPE.

Cooperative linkage arrangements have evolved in response to fiscal constraints and practical concerns for developing more efficient CPE delivery systems. As the interrelationships of professional organizations, employing agencies, and universities in CPE delivery become more clearly defined, increasing demands will be placed upon the program planner to develop skills in interorganization relations and the effective management of often complex linkage arrangements. Successful orchestration of such arrangements will no doubt improve the ability of planners to identify and reach the hard-to-reach professional.

The growth of CPE regulatory and accrediting mechanisms presents a different challenge to program planners. The often explicit accreditation requirements for traditional formats will discourage many from implementing nontraditional delivery systems. Lack of reciprocity between standards and credit equivalents of CPE accrediting agencies will often preclude interdisciplinary programming, and emphasis on participant "time served" as a basis for awarding recognition could supplant efforts to utilize outcome criteria as the basis for determining program effectiveness. The challenge to the planner attempting to attract the hard-to-reach professional will be to offer flexible and innovative programming within such systems of regulation.

Requirements for mandatory participation in CPE will surely have the most dramatic effect upon individuals and agencies responsible for continuing education programming. Reluctant professionals required to participate will be equally reluctant to learn unless the programming is relevant to their special characteristics and addresses their often different needs. The challenge will be to avoid succumbing to "production line" formats expediently designed to meet minimal requirements for participation, but instead to continue to design and implement programming appropriate to the various clienteles served.

References

Arndt, J. R., DeMuth, J. E., and Weinswig, M. H. "Participation of Wisconsin Pharmacists in Continuing Education, 1969–1973: A Preliminary Report." *American Journal of Pharmaceutical Education,* 1975, *39* (8), 264–266.

Bennett, N. "A Method for Continuing Education Program Development in a Semirural Setting." *Journal of Allied Health,* 1979, *8* (1), 34–37.

Bevis, M. E. "The Continuing Learning Activities of Neophyte Nurses." *Adult Education,* 1975, *25* (3), 169–191.

Broski, C., and Upp, S. C. "What Allied Health Professionals Want From Their Continuing Education Programs: A Study of Five Disciplines." *Journal of Allied Health,* 1979, *8* (1), 24–28.

Burgess, G. R. "Self-Esteem and Career Aspiration among Nurse Participants of Continuing Education." *Journal of Continuing Education in Nursing,* 1976, *7* (2), 7–12.

Castle, C. H., and Storey, P. "Physician Needs and Interests in Continuing Medical Education." *Journal of the American Medical Association,* 1968, *206* (3), 611–614.

Chamberlain, M. (Ed). *New Directions for Continuing Education: Providing Continuing Education by Media and Technology,* no. 5. San Francisco: Jossey-Bass, 1980.

Charters, A. N., and Blakely, R. J. "The Management of Continuing Learning: A Model of Continuing Education as a Problem-Solving Strategy for Health Manpower." In A. N. Charters and R. J. Blakely (Eds.), *Fostering the Growing Need to Learn: Monographs and Annotated Bibliography on Continuing Education and Health Manpower.* Syracuse, N.Y.: Syracuse University and the Regional Medical Program Service, Public Health Service, Department of Health, Education and Welfare, 1974.

Clark, K. M., and Dickinson, G. "Self-Directed and Other-Directed Continuing Education: A Study of Nurses' Participation." *Journal of Continuing Education in Nursing,* 1976, *7* (4), 16–24.

Denne, K. T., and others. "Mass Communications Media in Continuing Education." *Journal of Medical Education,* 1972, *47* (9), 712–716.

Gross, S. M. "A Study of the Relationship of Continuing Pharmaceutical Education to Selected Demographic, Attitudinal, and Competence-Related Criteria." Unpublished doctoral dissertation, Teachers College, Columbia University, 1975.

Hiemstra, R., and Long, R. "A Survey of Felt Versus Real Needs of Physical Therapists." *Adult Education,* 1974, *24* (4), 270–279.

Knowles, M. S. *The Modern Practice of Adult Education.* New York: Association Press, 1970.

Knox, A. B. "Lifelong Self-Directed Education." In A. N. Charters and R. J. Blakely (Eds.), *Fostering the Growing Need to Learn: Monographs and Annotated Bibliography on Continuing Education and Health Manpower.* Syracuse, N.Y.: Syracuse University and the Regional Medical Programs Service, Public Health Service, Department of Health, Education and Welfare, 1974.

Knox, A. B. "The Nature and Causes of Professional Obsolescence." In P. P. Le Breton and others (Eds.), *The Evaluation of Continuing Education for Professionals: A Systems View.* Seattle: Continuing Education, University of Washington, 1979a.

Knox, A. B. (Ed.). *New Directions for Continuing Education: Assessing the Impact of Continuing Education,* no. 3. San Francisco: Jossey-Bass, 1979b.

Kubat, J. "Correlates of Professional Obsolescence." *Journal of Continuing Education in Nursing,* 1975, *6* (6), 22–29, and 1976, *7* (1), 18–22.

Le Breton, P. P. and others. *The Evaluation of Continuing Education for Professionals: A Systems View.* Seattle: Continuing Education, University of Washington, 1979.

Lewis, C. E., and Hassanein, R. S. "Continuing Medical Education — An Epidemiological Evaluation." *New England Journal of Medicine,* 1970, *282* (4), 254–259.

Lloyd, J. S., and Abrahamson, S. "Effectiveness of Continuing Medical Education: A Review of the Evidence." *Evaluation and the Health Professions,* 1979, *2* (3), 251–280.

Manning, P. R. and others. "Continuing Medical Education: Linking the Community Hospital and the Medical School." *Journal of Medical Education,* 1979, *54* (6), 461–466.

Meyer, T. *A Feasibility Study in Determining Individual Practice Profiles of Physicians as a Basis for Continuing Education of These Physicians Utilizing a Postgraduate Preceptor Technique, Final Report.* Madison: University of Wisconsin, 1970.

Morgan, V. "A Study of Comparison of Independent Learning Activities Versus Attendance at Staff Development by Staff Nurses." *Journal of Continuing Education in Nursing,* 1977, *8* (3), 14–21.

Nakamoto, J., and Verner, C. *Continuing Education in the Health Professions — A Review of* the Literature: 1960–1970. Syracuse, N.Y.: ERIC Clearinghouse on Adult Education, 1973.

National Center for Education Statistics. *Participation in Adult Education: Final Report, 1975.* Washington, D.C.: U.S. Government Printing Office, 1978.

Owens, J. C., and others. "Continuing Education for the Rural Physician." *Journal of the American Medical Association,* 1979, *241* (12), 1261–1263.

Pennington, F. (Ed.). *New Directions for Continuing Education: Assessing Educational Needs of Adults,* no. 6. San Francisco: Jossey-Bass, 1980.

Schein, E. H. *Professional Education—Some New Directions.* New York: McGraw-Hill, 1972.

Smorynski, H. W., and Parochka, J. "Providing Continuing Education Opportunities in the Allied Health Professions." *Journal of Allied Health,* 1979, *8* (1), 47–54.

U.S. Department of Health, Education and Welfare. *The Supply of Health Manpower: 1970 Profiles and Projections to 1990.* Washington, D.C.: U.S. Government Printing Office, 1974.

Craig L. Scanlan is an assistant professor in the School of Allied Health Professions, College of Medicine and Dentistry of New Jersey, and associate director of the graduate program in allied health education, Graduate School of Education, Rutgers University.

A review of research and practice with strategies for increasing the participation of older adults in continuing education.

Overcoming the Age Bias in Continuing Education

Barbara Spencer

The 1971 White House Conference on Aging stressed the need for life-long learning and called for provision of a full range of educational opportunities for all older Americans. Although recognizing the particular promise of specific institutions, such as community colleges and community schools, the Conference's Section on Education noted explicitly that "all agencies with education as a part-time or full-time objective should be regarded as potential contributors to education for aging" (McCluskey, 1973, p. 5). Yet a decade later, despite increased awareness and considerable private and public support, the educational needs of the majority of older adults remain unmet. This failure to realize the full potential of continuing education for older persons is attributable in large part to several significant barriers to participation and to widespread failure to develop programs and recruitment strategies to overcome them. This chapter discusses the factors that inhibit participation in continuing education by the elderly and suggests approaches to comprehensive program planning and development designed to surmount them.

The Older Adult Problem

In 1975 approximately 22.4 million Americans were sixty-five years of age or older, representing 10.5 percent of the national population (U.S. Bureau of the Census, 1976). More importantly, during the last decade the impact of the postwar baby boom has passed, and the ratio of people aged sixty-five years and over to those under fifteen years has increased significantly. Educators must expect that, given a continued low fertility rate, the median age of the population will continue to increase.

Also noteworthy are trends and patterns within the group over sixty-five (U.S. Bureau of the Census, 1976). In 1975, 61.9 percent of the aged were sixty-five to seventy-four years of age, 29.7 percent were seventy-five to eighty-four, and 8.4 percent were eighty-five years or older. Among these categories, that of eighty-five or older was the fastest-growing. This suggests the relevance of attempts to differentiate among subgroups of the aged, such as the young old and old old.

The lack of an adequate income is one factor uniting the majority of older Americans. Although some elderly are well-to-do, and a considerable proportion are comfortable, the large majority face a harsh struggle for economic survival. In 1974, the median income for males over sixty-five was $4,535; the corresponding figure for women was $2,375 (U.S. Bureau of the Census, 1976). Income for specific subgroups, such as nonwhites, tended to be even lower. While it is true that old age does provide some economic benefits, such as added tax deductions and government-supported health programs, disadvantages outweigh advantages. For the vast majority of older persons, the combination of reliance on fixed incomes and recent inflationary pressures has contributed to a diminishing economic status.

Perhaps of greatest interest to adult educators is the previous educational experience of older people. In general, today's aged population has had less formal education than younger age groups (U.S. Bureau of the Census, 1976). In 1975, the median school years completed was nine for those sixty-five and over. Thus nearly half had not had any high school education. In fact, only one-third were high school graduates. Conversely, approximately one-fifth of all older adults were functionally illiterate. It should be noted, however, that the educational attainments of this age group will change considerably over the next several decades. Persons presently from forty-five to sixty-four years old have had significantly more formal education. Thus there will have to be a changing focus to continuing education for older adults as the educational skills and needs of this group change.

Education and the Older Adult

Expressions of concern for the educational needs of older adults often produce surprise and skepticism from those not actively in the field. This is largely the result of negative stereotypes concerning the needs and abilities of the elderly. Although there is some appreciation of the need for leisure-time education, society continues to overlook the rich potential of continuing education for older Americans. Many feel that those past sixty-five do not really want education, that they are self-absorbed and more concerned with the past than with acquiring new knowledge. Equally prevalent is the belief that older adults are more interested in entertainment, such as bingo and card playing, than substantive learning activities.

In addition, many doubt the ability of older adults to participate successfully in those educational programs that might inspire their interest. The view of old age as a period of rigidity, inflexibility and decreasing mental acuity is accepted too easily. Other related stereotypes contribute to this problem. Perceptions of the aged as weak and infirm, physically immobile, and terrified of the world around them hardly inspire confidence in educational programs devoted to the elderly.

Contrary to such portrayals, the educational needs and abilities of older adults provide considerable potential for continuing education. Several researchers, most notably McCluskey (1974), have made a convincing case for specific educational needs of the elderly. These are described below.

Coping Needs. Perhaps the most central educational need of older persons relates to the requirements of maintaining adequate social, physical, and psychological well-being. Included in this category are both basic educational and more specialized proficiencies needed for people to function as self-sustaining members of society; these needs could be met by health education and knowledge of legal and financial matters.

Influence Needs. These can be viewed as the procreative component of coping needs. That is, rather than just cope with situations that confront them, older adults feel the need to shape, at least partially, the world in which they live. As McCluskey (1971, p. 336) has noted, older persons have a "need to become agents of social change, and therefore a need for the kind of educational experience which will enable them to effectively and responsibly assume this role."

Expressive Needs. This category includes the need to participate in enjoyable activities judged to have intrinsic value. Such activity is characteristically spontaneous and allows for fulfillment of interests that have been unexpressed or underexpressed in earlier life. Liberal education, physical education, and hobbies fall within this area.

Contributive Needs. These arise from the personal belief that older persons have something to give, from the desire to be useful and to be wanted. This suggests participation in educational activities in which older adults not only learn but also impart specific skills or broader wisdom to other learners, whether fellow elders or younger persons.

Need for Transcendence. Older adults have a strong need for continued growth, a need to become more knowledgeable, worthwhile, and accomplished persons, both as individuals and as contributors to the lives of others. Learning devoted to this goal enables one to transcend declining physical abilities and diminishing life expectancies, and experience a sense of fulfillment in the later years.

In addition to revealing these educational needs, recent studies emphasize that older adults do have the ability to learn, and provide evidence that past research may have portrayed a false picture of the learning capabilities of the aged. The debate over the appropriateness of specific mental measurement procedures for the elderly has existed for some time, but several works now indicate that, given the proper setting or situation, age is a relatively unimportant barrier to learning (Arenberg and Robertson, 1974; Birren and Woodruff, 1973; Labouvie-Vief, 1976). People who keep alert and interested throughout life can expect little, if any, decline in intellectual ability. This is not to say that no decrements occur. Those abilities which involve speed, memory, or perception may decline over time. More important for continuing education, however, those abilities that depend on verbal comprehension, social awareness, or the application of experience show little or no loss and can even show slight gains (Labouvie-Vief, 1976).

Nevertheless, numerous studies conducted over a period of years demonstrate that participation in continuing education activities is inversely related to age. That is, older adults tend to be underrepresented among formal continuing education participants. Yet older persons are engaged in learning activities. As Hiemstra (1976) has noted, many elderly people undertake self-directed learning projects. However, the challenge remains for continuing educators to reach out to those who are not self-motivated.

During the last decade there have been many efforts in this direction. Recent surveys show that approximately one-third of the nation's colleges and universities offer special programs for older people (Scanlon, 1978). In addition, DeCrow (1975) reported that over 3,500 agencies, such as libraries, unions, museums, and community centers, provide continuing education opportunities for seniors. Despite this considerable range of programming, the participation rate for older Americans remains low. National statistics show that less than 3 percent of those over sixty participate in organized educational activities (National Center for Education Statistics, 1978).

More importantly, one should ask which older adults are participating in what types of educational programs. There has been considerable success with programs appealing to the younger, better-educated, and more affluent segment of the aged population. A prime example is the Elderhostel Movement, in which older adults participate in residential liberal arts programs at college and university campuses (Scanlon, 1978). Special programs geared to a specific segment of the aged population, such as the program for retired professionals at the New School for Social Research in New York City, have also prospered (Tenenbaum, 1979).

There has also been a burgeoning of community-based programs devoted to the expressive needs of older adults. Such programs, which attract a larger and more varied range of participants, most frequently stress hobbies and other leisure-time activities.

These trends suggest several dimensions to the unmet educational needs of older adults. Most basic is the need to increase overall levels of participation. The fact that fewer than one in thirty older adults take part in educational programs indicates the vast potential for increased involvement. Secondly, there is a need for programs designed to meet the full range of educational needs. Existing programs frequently fail to challenge learners, and do not address coping, influence, and transcendence needs. Lastly, there must be a concerted effort to attract the hard-to-reach, including such groups as the very old, the undereducated, the poor, minorities, the handicapped and physically infirm, the institutionalized, the rural elderly, and the socially isolated.

Barriers to Participation

A variety of factors account for low participation rates by adults of any age in continuing education activities. Informational, situational, institutional, and attitudinal barriers affect all potential participants to some degree. Yet it has been argued convincingly that these barriers have their greatest impact on older persons, a fact that serves to explain why this segment of the population is the most underrepresented in adult education enrollments.

Informational Barriers. Effective publicity campaigns are an essential part of successful educational programming. Unfortunately, as Darkenwald's introduction to this volume indicated, there is often inadequate awareness of continuing education resources in the community. Studies have shown that many adults of all ages have little knowledge of local opportunities for learning or where to go or whom to ask for such information. This problem is especially acute among older adults. Many aspects of later life — physical difficulties, changing work and family roles, loss of friends and loved ones — tend to narrow the older adult's social world, thus making it more difficult to reach the potential participant. That many providers of education for older adults rely on traditional methods of recruitment and publicity compounds this situation. Experience in the social service fields, such as health care and welfare, has demonstrated that concerted and innovattive efforts are required to open channels of communication to the hard-to-reach older adult (Trager, 1976).

Situational Barriers. Health problems represent a major barrier to participation. Older persons tend to be more afflicted with chronic conditions such as high blood pressure, heart trouble, or arthritis. Three out of four older adults experience such problems. Declining perceptual capabilities also trouble many of the elderly. It has been estimated that over one-half of all older persons experience some visual impairment. Similar patterns hold for hearing (Oyer, Kapur, and Deal, 1976). This does not mean that all older adults suffer such difficulties or that those who do are incapable of coping with such decrements. Nevertheless, it has been shown that health-related problems are a major limiting factor (Goodrow, 1975).

Mobility is also a key situational factor, because educational programming is useful and attractive only to the extent that it is accessible. Health problems are an obvious limit on mobility. Perhaps more important, however, is the frequent lack of safe, efficient, and inexpensive public transportation. Although there have been innovative attempts to provide special transportation services or reduced fares for older persons, many continue to cite lack of transportation as a most serious limitation (Goodrow, 1975; Monk, 1977). Related to these barriers is fear of crime. Many older persons, particularly those with physical impairments, feel themselves to be particularly vulnerable to criminal attack (National Council on the Aging, 1975).

Competing demands on available time are often cited as a significant constraint on participation (Goodrow, 1975; Hiemstra, 1972; Sarvis, 1973). Family responsibilities, housekeeping, assistance to friends, and contacts with service agencies detract from the time many older adults can devote to education. Responsibilities that are erratic or occur at irregular intervals inhibit participation in continuing education programs requiring strict scheduling or regular attendance.

Institutional Barriers. In some cases, specific program features can discourage participation of the aged. Scheduling is a prime example. Quite often educational programs for the elderly rely on facilities normally used for other purposes. This second-priority status frequently results in the need to schedule activities at times or in settings not ideally suited to older adults.

Program funding represents another serious problem. Although overhead costs may be assumed by the parent organization or the agency, operating costs generally must be covered by participant fees. This may discourage older learners with low incomes who view education as nonessential compared with other, more pressing expenses. Thus educational programming with regular fee schedules effectively limits participation to those with adequate means (Peterson, 1977).

Unfavorable physical conditions also hinder enrollment. Studies demonstrate that accessible, community-based programs experience the greatest success (McCluskey, 1978). However, centralized programs, such as those on college campuses, or programs quartered at inconvenient locations, can compound the transportation barrier, thereby discouraging attendance. Physical environment is also important. Facilities that lack elevators, wheelchair ramps, comfortable, well-lighted rooms, and other features appropriate to the physical needs of the elderly can reduce program effectiveness.

Lastly, complicated and depersonalized enrollment and registration procedures can have a negative impact. In-person registration, limited registration times, and detailed application forms can conflict with the abilities, desires, and time restraints of older adults.

Attitudinal Barriers. Older adults often possess attitudes, beliefs, perceptions, and values that discourage them from seeking continuing education. This is generally the result of accepting and internalizing the society's prevailing mythology of aging, with its negative stereotypes concerning the needs and abilities of older people.

Perhaps the most significant attitudinal barrier stems from the elderly's self-conceptions as poor learners. Many, reacting to images of the aged in the media and popular culture, portray themselves as "too old to learn"; others denigrate their physical abilities with statements such as "I don't have the energy" or "That takes too much effort." Such perceptions may be reinforced by an unfavorable prior educational experience. The fact that two-thirds of the aged lack a high school diploma, in a society that increasingly places emphasis on academic credentials, contributes to feelings of intellectual inadequacy. Not surprisingly, those who look upon their lack of educational attainment with embarrassment often avoid involvement in new activities that might rekindle feelings of inferiority (Goodrow, 1975).

A different aspect of this problem is ignorance of the nature and variety of continuing education opportunities. When older persons think of learning programs for adults, many think of formal, certificate-oriented programs, usually higher education, with admission standards, technical or detailed subject matter, rigorous course requirements, and testing. Thus many older persons perceive continuing education as an alien and even hostile world in which they are unwelcome and will not succeed.

Lastly, one must assess the response of older adults to continuing education within the larger sociocultural milieu of aging. Rather than being a time of promise and fulfillment, old age often becomes a time of struggle in an increasingly hostile world. Financial resources, often tied to a fixed income, begin to dwindle, especially in the face of inflation. Health may deteriorate. Crises related to role changes, loss of loved ones, social isolation, and other personal problems may precipitate an extreme sense of helplessness. Anxieties attendant upon these crises, reinforced by the mythology of aging, can strongly interfere with an older person's ability to function effectively in a variety of everyday situations. Continuing education for older adults cannot escape this context. Indeed, this represents a major paradox for practitioners in the field. While participation rates suffer as a result of this syndrome, continuing education remains one of the most promising means of helping older persons to overcome their anxieties and enjoy increased self-esteem and fulfillment.

Reaching Out: Successful Programming for the Older Adult

Structuring Programs. Educational programs for older adults should be direct, personal, and accessible. Directness requires a programmatic presence within the community. Consequently, the sponsoring institution must make contact with potential participants within the context of their daily lives. A program is personal when it conveys an interest in the potential learners as persons and individuals, and when learners can relate comfortably to the provider organization. Accessibility is achieved through a flexible program structure and administrative practices that anticipate and limit the negative impact of situational and institutional barriers.

A variety of strategies can be used to develop educational programs with these characteristics. Most basic is the commitment to outreach, a comprehensive effort to reach beyond the physical, perceptual, and personal boundaries of the "home" institution. Successful outreach efforts provide new allies, new locales, new approaches, and new learners.

Although a single organization can conduct outreach efforts independently, by renting a storefront or sending representatives directly into the community, it is more effective to employ some form of social linkage (Beder and Smith, 1977). Linkage involves cooperation between or among organizations in which resources are exchanged. There is a full range of linkage relationships, from single or occasional reliance on another organization for a specific resource, such as a mailing list, to formal cosponsorship with an agency sharing a complementary mission or commitment to the same group of learners. The organizations with which a sponsor of educational programs for older adults might form linkage relationships include:

1. Government agencies, such as the federal Administration on Aging (AOA), the Social Security Administration, county departments of health and social services, state and local departments for the aging, and other locally designated sponsors for senior-oriented programs

(Meals on Wheels, Nutrition Sites, Senior Companions, Retired Senior Volunteer Program, local departments of parks and recreation that conduct recreation programs for the elderly, and the public libraries).

2. Economic organizations, such as businesses and industries (especially banks and small retailers, unions, and local branches of organizations for professionals, including doctors, lawyers, nurses and dieticians, and farmers' cooperatives).

3. Educational institutions, such as public schools, community continuing education programs, community schools, community colleges and universities, the Cooperative Extension Service, educational television stations, and other sponsors of educational programs for older adults.

4. Cultural agencies, such as public libraries, museums, zoos, botanical gardens, and arts councils.

5. Health and welfare organizations, such as the Salvation Army, the Red Cross, the Legal Aid Society, the Visiting Nurses Association, tenant organizations, and organizatons devoted to the cure and treatment of specific diseases, including cancer, arthritis, or glaucoma.

6. Civic, neighborhood, and fraternal societies, such as the Elks, Lions, Rotary, Knights of Columbis, Masons, B'nai B'rith, local chambers of commerce, the Grange, all forms of the "Y," veterans' organizations, settlement houses, and neighborhood centers.

7. Religious groups, such as churches and synagogues, auxiliaries, societies, and Bible study groups.

8. Senior advocacy groups, such as Gray Panthers, local chapters of such groups as the American Assocation of Retired Persons, the National Retired Teachers Association, the Retired Telephone Workers, the National Council of Senior Citizens, and Federation of Senior Citizens.

9. Institutions serving the elderly, such as retirement communities, senior congregate housing, acute-care hospitals, nursing homes, mobile-home parks, senior citizen centers and single-room occupancy residences.

As the number and diversity of organizations within a linkage network increase, the role of each organization may become more specialized. A matrix of groups and resources results, with members drawing upon specific organizations for specialized assistance. The product is a pool of resources, such as facilities, funding, technical equipment, staff skills, means of transportation, mailing and membership lists, and referral services, that is larger and more varied than that of any one network member.

Linkage is of particular value in reaching out to recruit program participants. Cooperation with existing organizations, each with contacts and credibility within the community, enables the program provider to make a direct and personal approach to groups of older adults. Methods of recruitment include but are in no way restricted to the following:

Mass Media. Although somewhat depersonalized and one-dimensional, television (including cable TV), radio, and newspapers provide the opportunity to reach large numbers of older persons. Studies show that many of the elderly spend a considerable portion of their time watching television, making this an effective method for publicizing educational programs (Rush and Kent, 1976).

Special Announcements. Means of communication, usually printed, that are owned by or directed at specific groups allow better targeting of recruitment efforts. Examples of such materials include newsletters published by local senior citizen or golden age clubs, bulletins of organizations with substantial numbers of older adults, such as unions or veterans' groups, all forms of the "Y," bulletins of religious organizations, and company newspapers, which are often sent to retired employees. One may also request the assistance of corporations that make large, periodic mailings, such as telephone and utility companies. These companies generally include public service or public relations announcements with their bills, and can advertise an educational program with little effort.

Brochures and Posters. Although some older adults may be socially isolated or experience limited mobility, the vast majority do frequent such locations as grocery stores, pharmacies, banks, and post offices. These heavy-traffic areas are excellent distribution points for posters or brochures advertising educational programs. Many stores and banks even provide public bulletin boards suitable for this purpose. In addition, cooperative store owners, pharmacists, bank employees, and others can greatly improve such recruitment efforts by dispensing brochures or other handouts to their elderly patrons.

Personal Contact. Face-to-face recruitment activity represents one of the most effective strategies, because it permits a dialogue between a program representative and potential participants. Presentations at organizations devoted primarily to older persons, such as senior citizen centers or retirees' clubs, are an ideal means of making contact. Information booths at supermarkets, banks, libraries, and shopping centers also have proved value. Telephone canvassing, using lists supplied by linkage partners, is particularly appropriate for reaching the homebound. Above all, one should not neglect the possibility of using older adults as recruiters; they serve as positive role models and are best suited to be supportive of hesitant participants.

The content of the recruitment message is as important as the method through which it is communicated. The way a program is portrayed can do much to overcome attitudinal and some situational barriers. Brochures and verbal presentations should include a full description of the program, covering such aspects as program goals, content, method of teaching, the location, and the number and schedule of sessions. Special arrangements designed to increase participation, such as the provision of transportation, should be underscored. Lastly, terminology that might have negative connotations should be avoided.

Accessibility, which is essential to overcoming situational and institutional barriers, is the product of sound program structure and administrative flexibility. It is critical that those planning the program know the characteristics of the target population and, to the extent possible, anticipate factors that may limit participation. The program site should be within reach of the potential participants. Where possible the program should be brought to them. Linkage relationships can often be used to procure a convenient site, which may be in a nontraditional location, such as a library, union hall, or health clinic. The site ultimately chosen should have facilities appropriate for older adults, such as comfortable chairs, adequate lighting, and elevators where necessary. Scheduling is another important component of program structure. The duration of each session and the total number of sessions should not be overly rigorous. The time chosen for sessions is even more critical, with knowledge of the participants' needs and common sense the key criteria. Fear of crime and visual impairments experienced by many older people suggest avoidance of evening activities. Classes on the first or second business day of the month may conflict with visits to the bank. As a last example, in certain parts of the country winter weather reduces turnout at educational programs.

If possible, the provision of transportation should be coordinated with the program, especially if the location or scheduling of sessions is not particularly favorable. Once again, linkage can be beneficial because many organizations have access to vans, buses, or minibuses. If necessary, carpools can be organized among the participants or volunteers. Such strategies are especially crucial if one is developing a program for the rural elderly.

As a final consideration, program fees should be kept as low as possible. By limiting or entirely eliminating the cost to learners, one opens up the program to participation by persons of lesser means. Cosponsorship offers an opportunity to acquire additional funding and achieve this goal.

Successful efforts to make a program accessible pay a double reward. While a larger number of adults are able to participate, the impact on attitudinal barriers can be equally important. When older persons see their needs anticipated and addressed, they feel welcome and less reticent to undertake new experiences.

Facilitating Learning. Overcoming informational, situational, and institutional barriers through successful recruitment and the design of an accessible program does not necessarily ensure that educational goals will be attained. Quite often negative self-images remain. Such attitudinal barriers are not removed by mere enrollment in a program. Rather, the ensuing learning experience should be one that helps to overcome continuing doubts and fears by providing a supportive and responsive environment. The quality of the learning experience will be the key factor in promoting the continued participation of the older adult and influencing whether the person is motivated to use the knowledge gained.

The educational approach formulated by Knowles (1970) is particularly appropriate for facilitating learning among the elderly. According to Knowles, the underlying conditions that characterize a positive learning climate are physical comfort, trust, respect, and helpfulness within the group. The climate supports the emergence of critical elements in the learning process. A formal classroom atmosphere should be avoided. The learners' desire for knowledge should be reinforced. There should be no discrepancy between the announced and evolving goals of the program and those of the participants. The learners should be given a share of the responsibility for planning and conducting learning activities. In this way the learners become active partners in the process while gaining in self-confidence and commitment to their goals. The concept of shared responsibility results in leaders who are facilitators, and who assist participants in self-directed learning, instead of teachers who simply present information. In addition, the learning process should be related to and draw upon the life experiences of the participants. Lastly, the program should be designed and structured so that each successive component builds upon previous learning to reinforce a sense of accomplishment and progress toward the learners' goals.

This type of learning experience, with its emphasis on participative planning and instruction, provides what Hixson (1969) has termed "nonthreatening education." In this supportive setting, the older adult is of primary importance and the content secondary. Where emphasis is placed on the involvement of the individual, the learning situation is more likely to foster self-actualization or transcendence. For the older adult, this concept represents "transcendence of the past, transcendence of previous social roles, and transcendence of a limited definition of the self" (Moody, 1978, p. 44). It calls for an educational experience that is truly unique; one that is worthy of devoting time to during the later years.

A Successful Program:
The Institute of Study for Older Adults

Since its inception in 1969, the Institute of Study for Older Adults, (ISOA) at New York City Community College, a program incorporating many of the concepts discussed here, has adhered closely to its original goals:

1. Bring education to our senior citizens in the communities.

2. Stimulate, train, and create an understanding among faculty and staff of community colleges in New York City to develop education programs and services for senior citizens in their communities.

3. Train the aged themselves to develop leaders to assume responsiblity for educational programs in collaboration with community colleges, neighborhood associations, and other agencies.

4. Conduct seminars and conferences with a variety of participants including our students, teachers, other educators, and public officials in order to study the needs of older adults for continuing education, improve the quality of our services to older adults, and help develop a pedagogy for the older adult.

The program offers a number of specific activities and services intended to meet the challenge set forth by these goals. These components include:

Liberal Arts Courses. Older people receive liberal arts instruction in senior centers, libraries, banks, residence homes, nursing homes, and other locations throughout New York City. Approximately 200 courses are held in over 100 locations, with registrations exceeding 5,000.

Ethnic Heritage Program. This program provides for the preparation of older adults as peer teachers in ethnic heritage studies. In addition, the seniors serve as school volunteers and offer courses in ethnic studies to sixth-grade students.

Consumer Education Program. Based on an extensive needs assessment study of the consumer needs of older adults, the program provides for the dissemination of consumer information by trained seniors.

Homebound Program. Older adults unable to leave their homes participate in educational discussions based upon television viewing with visiting education aides, often seniors themselves.

Information and Referral. Older persons and paraprofessionals attend seminars and workshops designed to review information and resource material relevant to the problems and needs of the elderly. The older persons then serve as volunteer information and referral counselors at their senior centers.

Retirement Education Training for Options in Optimal Living (RETOOL). ISOA contracts with employers to provide retirement educational programming and counseling.

The ISOA is essentially an outreach-oriented program. Virtually all learning activity takes place beyond the campus of New York City Community College. For the most part, courses and programs are offered at locations where older persons are concentrated, such as community centers, "Y"s, unions, libraries, hospitals, homes for the elderly, and senior centers. But as the description of the Homebound Program made clear, ISOA endeavors to bring education to all older adults. This is true not only for the homebound, but for the blind, deaf, and non-English speaking as well.

The wide range of ISOA programming is the result of a complex network of linkage relationships designed to recruit participants and obtain cosponsors. An advisory committee, composed of over two dozen representatives of government agencies, unions, local business, senior and neighborhood centers, and educational institutions serves as the nexus of this linkage network. The Institute is also the major force of a unique linkage among other community colleges in the New York metropolitan area. Faced with an increasing demand for its services, ISOA decided several years ago that it would be unwise to expand too far beyond its service area or the range of its resources. Rather, it began to assist other educational institutions by offering training and cosponsorship for similar programs in the city's other boroughs.

The Institute has a small central staff, which has little time for direct face-to-face recruitment of participants. Therefore, it relies upon its linkage partners for this aspect of program development. Once it is decided that a given senior center or other organization will host a program, the center director assumes a major coordinating role. An educational committee, composed of older persons, works with the director in assessing the needs and wishes of the potential participants, helping to select courses and recruit learners. In addition, the director and the educational committee decide on course schedules and the facilities to be used. By direct involvement of those most familiar with the center and its members, ISOA programs can provide an educational experience that addresses the unique needs of the learners.

Because of this "custom-tailored" approach, ISOA educational activities have high rates of completion and learner satisfaction. This becomes a major factor in recruitment, for many current registrants report participation in a previous course or program. In addition, those who enjoy the course are instrumental in recruiting additional participants.

The concept underlying all ISOA programs is that involvement in the learning process is as beneficial as the specific knowledge gained. By engaging in a meaningful learning experience, older adults maintain healthy and active minds and are better able to combat the mental atrophy and functional senility that can accompany aging. In Institute programs, seniors, assisted by college facilitators, assume responsibility for their own learning within an environment that stresses dialogue, group discussion, and peer teaching. Although courses are designed to be enjoyable and socially stimulating, the principal goal is a substantive educational experience. Thus the courses are intellectually challenging without being threatening. There are no tests or written assignments, nor are grades given. Rather, participants are encouraged to do outside work for their own benefit and the benefit of the other participants. Experience shows that this approach works; most students do indeed function as successful, self-directed learners. Lastly, the use of peer teaching and the subsequent use of participants as teachers in other programs such as ethnic studies provide positive role models for older adults. Not only do the courses provide a supportive opportunity to learn, but the total ISOA program offers numerous chances for successful participants to continue learning, as well as to serve recruiters, counselors, or teachers in their own right.

Continuing education should play a vital role in the lives of older Americans. Yet data on participation reveal that it does not. Ninety-seven percent of those sixty-five or over are not engaged in organized educational activity. Thus adult educators face the challenge of involving the aged population in education. As this chapter has indicated, the challenge cannot be met simply by better marketing. Rather, the very concepts underlying current programming for older persons must be reevaluated and new approaches developed and adopted. Strategies such as outreach and social linkage will have to be used to create a supportive environment that is accessible and that relates to the needs and abilities of older learners. Above all, the educational experience must be one that enhances the self-image of the participants and fosters self-directed learning. Only in this way will older adults view continuing education as a valuable and worthwhile endeavor.

References

Arenberg, D. L., and Robertson, E. A. "The Older Individual as a Learner." In S. M. Grabowski and W. D. Mason (Eds.), *Learning for Aging*. Washington, D.C.: Adult Education Association of the U.S.A., 1974.

Beder, H., and Smith, F. *Developing an Adult Education Program Through Community Linkages*. Washington, D.C.: Adult Education Association of the U.S.A., 1977.

Birren, J. E., and Woodruff, D. S. "Human Development over the Life Span through Education." In P. Baltes and W. Schaie (Eds.), *Life Span Developmental Psychology*. New York: Academic, 1973.

De Crow, R. *New Learning for Older Americans: An Overview of National Effort*. Washington, D.C.: Adult Education Association of the U.S.A., 1975.

Goodrow, B. A. "Limiting Factors in Reducing Participation in Older Adult Learning Opportunities." *The Gerontologist*, 1975, *15* (3), 418–422.

Heisel, M. A., Darkenwald, G. G., and Anderson, R. E. "Educational Participation Behavior of Adults 60 and Older." *Educational Gerontology* (forthcoming).

Hiemstra, R. "Continuing Education for the Aged: A Survey of Needs and Interests of Older People." *Adult Education*, 1972, *22* (2), 100–109.

Hiemstra, R. "The Older Adult's Learning Projects." *Educational Gerontology*, 1976, *1* (4), 331–341.

Hixson, L. E. "Nonthreatening Education for Older People." *Adult Leadership*, 1969, *18* (9), 84–85.

Knowles, M. *The Modern Practice of Adult Education*. New York: Association Press, 1970.

Labouvie-Vief, G. "Toward Optimizing Cognitive Competence in Later Life." *Educational Gerontology,* 1976, *1* (1), 75–92.

McCluskey, H. Y. "Education: Background and Issues." In *White House Conference on Aging.* Washington, D.C.: U.S. Government Printing Office, 1971.

McCluskey, H. Y. "Cochairman's Statement on Education." In *Toward a National Policy on Aging.* Washington, D.C.: U.S. Government Printing Office, 1973.

McCluskey, H. Y. "Education for Aging: The Scope of the Field and Perspectives for the Future." In S. M. Grabowski and W. D. Mason (Eds.), *Learning for Aging.* Washington, D.C.: Adult Education Association, 1974.

McCluskey, H. Y. "The Community of Generations: A Goal and a Context for the Education of Persons in the Later Years." In R. H. Sherron and D. B. Lumsden (Eds.), *Introduction to Educational Gerontology.* Washington, D.C.: Hemisphere, 1978.

Monk, A. "Education and the Rural Aged." *Educational Gerontology,* 1977, *2* (2), 147–156.

Moody, H. R. "Education and the Life Cycle: A Philosophy of Aging." In R. H. Sherron and D. B. Lumsden (Eds.), *Introduction to Educational Gerontology.* Washington, D.C.: Hemisphere, 1978.

National Center for Education Statistics. *Participation in Adult Education: Final Report, 1975.* Washington, D.C.: U.S. Government Printing Office, 1978.

National Council on the Aging. *The Myth and Reality of Aging in America.* Washington, D.C.: National Council on the Aging, 1975.

Oyer, H. Kapur, Y. and Deal, L. "Hearing Disorders in the Aging: Effects Upon Communication." In H. J. Oyer and E. J. Oyer (Eds.), *Aging and Communication.* Baltimore: University Park Press, 1976.

Peterson, D. A. "The Role of Gerontology in Adult Education." In R. A. Kalish (Ed.), *The Later Years: Social Applications of Gerontology.* Belmont, Calif.: Wadsworth, 1977.

Rush, R. R., and Kent, K. E. M. "Communication Channel Selection Considerations for Reaching Older Persons: Part I." *Educational Gerontology,* 1976, *1* (4), 379–390.

Sarvis, R. E. *Educational Needs of the Elderly: Their Relationships to Educational Institutions.* Washington, D.C.: National Center for Educational Research and Development, 1973.

Scanlon, J. *How to Plan a College Program for Older People.* New York: Academy for Educational Development, 1978.

Tenenbaum, F. *Over 55 Is Not Illegal.* Boston: Houghton Mifflin, 1979.

Trager, N. P. "Available Communication Networks for the Aged in the Community." In H. J. Oyer and E. J. Oyer (Eds.), *Aging and Communication.* Baltimore: University Park Press, 1976.

U.S. Bureau of the Census. "Demographic Aspects of Aging and the Older Population in the United States." In *Current Population Reports,* Series P-23, no. 59. Washington, D.C.: U.S. Government Printing Office, 1976.

Barbara Spencer, formerly an educational manager at Citicorp and coordinator of the graduate program in educational gerontology at Rutgers University, is assistant professor of adult and continuing education at Teachers College, Columbia University.

Who are hard-to-reach adults? Why are they hard to reach?
And what can we do to reach them?

What We Know About Reaching Hard-to-Reach Adults

Gordon G. Darkenwald
Gordon A. Larson

This volume has brought together authors with varied backgrounds to set forth the state of the art in reaching hard-to-reach adult populations. In this concluding chapter an effort will be made to summarize the concepts and practical suggestions offered by these authors and come to some conclusions regarding what we know about reaching the hard-to-reach.

Who Are the Hard-to-Reach?

In this sourcebook the hard-to-reach have been described from three different perspectives. Darkenwald emphasized statistical representation, which is the perspective taken by many administrators and policymakers. The hard-to-reach are identified as groups that are underrepresented as participants in continuing education activities. From this standpoint, the hard-to-reach are the elderly, the isolated, the handicapped, and persons of low socioeconomic status (particularly those of low educational attainment). Irish and Spencer employed a similar perspective in their chapters dealing with reaching these groups.

As Darkenwald notes, however, the statistical approach is only one way of defining the hard-to-reach. From the marketing perspective, described by Beder, the hard-to-reach adult may be anyone whom the continuing education agency wishes to reach who does not participate. Beder suggests that the hard-to-reach may be considered as one segment of the potential continuing education market, a segment sharing certain characteristics that lead them not to participate. This analytical framework avoids the pitfall of stereotyping the hard-to-reach as coming only from specific ethnic, economic, or social groups within society. It permits us, for example, to consider businesspersons or professionals who do not participate as hard to reach, even though they are not part of a population that is generally underrepresented in continuing education. An advantage of the marketing viewpoint is that it forces one to examine the characteristics that relate to nonparticipation across all groups, rather than just within those specific groups that have been hardest to reach as a whole.

Scanlan offers a third perspective on this subject. While the statistical approach used by Darkenwald and the marketing approach used by Beder both define the hard-to-reach in terms of nonparticipation, Scanlan notes that from the public's perspective the real issue is more than participation or nonparticipation. Instead, for professionals, it is whether or not they maintain technical competence. This perspective requires that we go beyond counting heads in the continuing education classroom and take a deeper look at alternative forms of participation and the reasons why certain people choose not to participate. Scanlan has identifed three broad categories of nonparticipants in continuing professional education: the pacesetters, who keep ahead of the field and for whom continuing education, in a traditional sense, is largely irrelevant; the would-be participants, who are constrained by barriers to participation; and the true laggards, who lack the motivation to continue their professional education.

Why Are They Hard to Reach?

Darkenwald provides the major theoretical perspective on why certain people are hard to reach in his concept of barriers. This theme, echoed by the other authors, posits for general types of barriers: informational, attitudinal, situational, and institutional. In order for adults to participate in continuing education, they must be aware of the existence of the program, must be motivated to participate, and must be willing to surmount problems caused by their environment or created by the provider institution which militate against participation. It is important to note here that all of these factors must be considered in order to achieve the final goal of increasing participation among the hard-to-reach. All too often, analysis focuses on only one reason or one cluster of reasons for nonparticipation, resulting in simplistic and ineffective attempts at solutions. Thus, any advice on how to reach the hard-to-reach must be preceded with the caveat that there are no simple solutions or formulas for success that can be applied to all situations.

How Can We Reach Them?

As Darkenwald notes, there are at least four different models for addressing the participation problem. The economic model suggests that the educator has only to examine all the costs and benefits of continuing education and ensure that the benefits exceed the costs and are perceived that way by the target population. This model assumes that people act rationally in deciding whether or not to participate. It also fails to consider forces other than economic ones impinging upon the decision.

The force field model considers a broader range of psychological, social, and environmental forces operating on the individual and suggests that certain groups do not participate because the impact of negative forces exceeds that of positive ones. The continuing educator must try to minimize those forces that are negative and enhance those that are positive.

The congruence model suggests that participation will be maximized when the learning environment is made more congruent with the characteristics of a specific hard-to-reach group. As an example, literacy classes for factory workers are more likely to attract participants if they are held in the work environment rather than a formal school setting.

The expectancy-valence model recognizes that the decision to participate, although affected by social forces, is an individual one and that two factors, valence and expectancy, must be manipulated to promote participation. Valence may be seen as a force field analysis applied on an individual basis. The individual must believe that the positive benefits to be gained from participation outweigh the negative. Expectancy relates to the individual's perception of potential for success. Not only must individuals see the value of participation, but they must also feel that they have a reasonable probability both of participating and achieving their intended purposes.

The theoretical models are important because they provide a framework for evaluating the reasons for success and failure of various programs and techniques, but they do not offer concrete suggestions that can be employed by the practitioner. Beder's marketing approach is more useful in that regard. It offers a general step-by-step method of program development that can be applied to a variety of situations. As Beder notes, conventional marketing techniques have limitations when applied to the problem of reaching the hard-to-reach. One of the main reasons that certain individuals and groups are hard to reach is that they do not respond to the normal marketing strategies employed by continuing educators.

A key element of success in reaching hard-to-reach populations is discussed in Larson's chapter on communications and is amplified by Irish, Spencer, and Scanlan in their discussions of reaching specific groups. For reasons discussed in these chapters, the mass media by themselves have proved to be inadequate for reaching the hard-to-reach. While the mass media have potential for increasing awareness and interest and for rapidly disseminating information, their use must be supplemented by more personal approaches to communication. One of the reasons for this is that the hard-to-reach need a great deal of persuasion and encouragement to initiate and sustain participation.

A recurrent theme expressed by the authors is that recruiting activities must be coupled with well-designed and innovative programming techniques in order to attract and sustain participation among the hard-to-reach groups. Case studies provided by Irish, Spencer, and Scanlan illustrate this assertion. A corollary of this theme is that the problem must be seen as multifaceted and complex, requiring a wide range of carefully designed and orchestrated interventions to encourage sustained and effective participation.

Clearly, we have learned a good deal about reaching the hard-to-reach adult. However, this volume can only provide general guidelines and perspectives to be built upon and refined by individual continuing educators whose problems and needs are situation-specific. The references cited in each chapter can provide additional information that may be useful in this regard. In addition, several works are worthy of special note.

For Further Study

This volume summarizes the state of the art of reaching the hard-to-reach adult, drawing on the work of scholars from many disciplines and specific areas of inquiry. For those who may wish to explore the basic scholarship in greater depth, the following references are suggested.

As noted in Chapter One, the primary explanatory theories of participation are Boshier's (1973) congruence model, Dhanidina and Griffith's (1975) cost-benefit model, Miller's (1967) force field analysis, and Rubenson's (1977) valence-expectancy model. The most useful treatment of the marketing concept as applied to education is found in Kotler (1975). Two comprehensive works dealing with the communication process are Havelock (1971) and Rogers and Shoemaker (1971). For practical suggestions on reaching the least educated and most in need, readers are referred to *Last Gamble on Education* (Mezirow, Darkenwald, and Knox, 1975) and *Adult Illiteracy in the United States* (Hunter and Harmon, 1979). Two major sources of information on continuing professional education are the review of the literature by Nakamoto and Verner (1973) and the collections of papers by Le Breton and others (1979) and by Charters and Blakely (1974). Finally, for more information on reaching the older population, see *Learning for Aging* (Grabowski and Mason, 1974).

References

Boshier, R. W. "Educational Participation and Dropout: A Theoretical Model." *Adult Education,* 1973, *23* (4), 255–282.

Charters, A. N., and Blakley, R. J. (Eds.). *Fostering the Growing Need to Learn: Monographs and Annotated Bibliography on Continuing Education and Health Manpower.* Syracuse, N.Y.: Syracuse University, 1974.

Dhanidina, L., and Griffith, W. S. "Costs and Benefits of Delayed High School Completion." *Adult Education,* 1975, *25* (4), 217–230.

Grabowski, S. M., and Mason, W. D. (Eds.). *Learning for Aging.* Washington, D.C.: Adult Education Association, 1974.

Havelock, R. G. *Planning for Innovation Through Dissemination and Utilization of Knowledge.* Ann Arbor, Mich.: Center for Research on Utilization of Scientific Knowledge, 1971.

Hunter, C. S., and Harman, D. *Adult Illiteracy in the United States.* New York: McGraw-Hill, 1979.

Kotler, P. *Marketing for Nonprofit Organizations.* Englewood Cliffs, N.J.: Prentice-Hall, 1975.

Le Breton, P. P. and others (Eds.). *The Evaluation of Continuing Education for Professionals: A Systems View.* Seattle: Continuing Education, University of Washington, 1979.

Mezirow, J., Darkenwald, G. G., and Knox, A. *Last Gamble on Education: Dynamics of Adult Basic Education.* Washington, D.C.: Adult Education Association, 1975.

Miller, H. L. *Participation of Adults in Education: A Force Field Analysis.* Boston: Center for the Study of Liberal Education for Adults, 1967.

Nakamoto, J., and Verner, C. *Continuing Education in the Health Professions: A Review of the Literature, 1960–1970.* Syracuse, N.Y.: ERIC Clearinghouse on Adult Education, 1973.

Rogers, E. M., and Shoemaker, F. *Communication of Innovations.* New York: Free Press, 1971.

Rubenson, K. *Participation in Recurrent Education.* Paris: Center for Educational Research and Innovation, Organization for Economic Cooperation and Development, 1977.

Gordon G. Darkenwald is associate professor of adult and continuing education and codirector, Center for Adult Development, Graduate School of Education, Rutgers University.

Gordon A. Larson is assistant professor of adult education and reading and codirector, Center for Adult Development, Graduate School of Education, Rutgers University.

Index

New Directions Quarterly Sourcebooks

New Directions for Continuing Education is one of several distinct series of quarterly sourcebooks published by Jossey-Bass. The sourcebooks in each series are designed to serve both as *convenient compendiums* of the latest knowledge and practical experience on their topics and as *long-life reference tools.*

One-year, four-sourcebook subscriptions for each series cost $18 for individuals (when paid by personal check) and $30 for institutions, libraries, and agencies. Single copies of earlier sourcebooks are available at $6.95 each *prepaid* (or $7.95 each when *billed*).

A complete listing is given below of current and past sourcebooks in the *New Directions for Continuing Education* series. The titles and editors-in-chief of the other series are also listed. To subscribe, or to receive further information, write: New Directions Subscriptions, Jossey-Bass Inc., Publishers, 433 California Street, San Francisco, California 94104.

New Directions for Continuing Education
Alan B. Knox, Editor-in-Chief
1979:   1. *Enhancing Proficiencies of Continuing Educators,*
            Alan B. Knox
        2. *Programming for Adults Facing Mid-Life Change,* Alan B. Knox
        3. *Assessing the Impact of Continuing Education,* Alan B. Knox
        4. *Attracting Able Instructors of Adults,* M. Alan Brown,
            Harlan G. Copeland
1980:   5. *Providing Continuing Education by Media and Technology,*
            Martin N. Chamberlain
        6. *Teaching Adults Effectively,* Alan B. Knox
        7. *Assessing Educational Needs of Adults,* Floyd C. Pennington

New Directions for Child Development
William Damon, Editor-in-Chief

New Directions for College Learning Assistance
Kurt V. Lauridsen, Editor-in-Chief

New Directions for Community Colleges
Arthur M. Cohen, Editor-in-Chief
Florence B. Brawer, Associate Editor

New Directions for Exceptional Children
James J. Gallagher, Editor-in-Chief